A DYLAN ODYSSEY

GRAFFEG

Published by Graffeg Limited
May 2015
ISBN 9781909823440

A Dylan Odyssey
Compiled by Literature Wales
Picture research by Jeff Towns
Illustrations and titles by Sarah Edmonds

Designed and produced by Graffeg

Graffeg Limited, 24 Stradey Park Business
Centre, Mwrwg Road, Llangennech,
Llanelli, Carmarthenshire SA14 8YP
Wales UK Tel 01554 824000
www.graffeg.com

Distributed by the Welsh Books
Council www.cllc.org.uk
castellbrychan@cllc.org.uk

A CIP Catalogue record for this book is
available from the British Library.

123456789

A DYLAN ODYSSEY

Follow in the steps of Dylan Thomas. 15 literary tours in Wales, Oxford, London and New York by Griff Rhys Jones, Hannah Ellis, Gillian Clarke and other writers and artists. Compiled by Literature Wales.

GRAFFEG

Contents

Foreword by Lleucu Siencyn

During the long hot summer of 2014, Literature Wales ran its 'A Dylan Odyssey' literary tour programme as part of the Dylan Thomas 100 Festival to celebrate the centenary year of Dylan Thomas' birth.

Each tour aimed to capture a place connected with Dylan Thomas, illustrating how his life and words were inextricably bound with the landscapes, people and cultures of Wales and beyond. Each tour offered a unique insight into the many faces of Dylan Thomas, enabling a greater understanding of the man and his writing.

The tours took us from his birth town in Swansea through to his final few days in Greenwich Village, New York, via Laugharne, New Quay, Oxford and Fitzrovia, London. Others explored themes in his work through place; mental health was scrutinised by the full moon in Criccieth, and surrealism and 1930s-50s popular culture were tracked through the galleries of the National Museum Cardiff.

Wales' contemporary writers set off on these journeys, exploring each place on foot and by horseback, horse and carriage, canoe, boat and bus. Enchanting, illuminating and enthralling the groups that went with them, each tour yielded a deeper context of meaning for those on board, and for the writers themselves.

This book captures the essence of each tour through the eyes of each writer, illustrated by gorgeous interpretive maps, photography and ephemera from Dylan's life. Readers can follow in the footsteps and mindmaps of Dylan Thomas. Each chapter is a visual and literary treat.

In these pages actor and comedian, Griff Rhys Jones, will lead you through the streets of Fitzrovia; National Poet of Wales, Gillian Clarke, will take you down the rural Carmarthenshire lanes of Dylan's childhood haunts by pony and trap; the former Archdruid, T. James Jones, explores the influence of the Welsh language on Dylan's work; his granddaughter

Hannah Ellis takes us back to family life at the Boathouse in Laugharne; and biographer Andrew Lycett travels through the myths and legends of Dylan let loose in Oxford.

Our hope is that this book will allow you to experience these tours for yourself again and again. Come to Wales. Come to the pubs, beaches, urbanscapes, heaths and leafy tracks of Dylan's worlds and experience the heart of our unique creative culture for yourself.

I hope you enjoy the journey.

Lleucu Siencyn
Literature Wales CEO

a map of A DYLAN ODYSSEY: Wales & Beyond

N NW NE W E SW SE S

Bangor

Snowdonia National Park

Wrexham

7 • Cricieth

ENGLAND

15 to Greenwich Village, NEW YORK

CARDIGAN BAY

• Aberystwyth

• Aberaeron

11 New Quay

cardigan

10 • Talsarn

BRECON Beacons National PARK

12 to OXFORD

5

Pembrokeshire Coast National Park

• BRONWYDD ARMS

• CARMARTHEN

Monmouth •

13 14 2 Laugharne

1 3 9 4 • SWANSEA

GOWER

Newport

8 to Fitzrovia LONDON

6 CARDIFF •

BRISTOL Channel

1. Dylan's Swansea Uplands
2. South Carmarthenshire
3. Swansea Hollywood
4. Gower and Mumbles
5. Welsh Language
6. Dylan Thomas and Organic Surrealism
7. Cricieth
8. London Fitzrovia
9. The Swansea Blitz
10. Caitlin Thomas' Aeron Valley
11. Ceredigion Coast
12. Oxford and South Leigh
13. Dylan Thomas' Laugharne
14. The Thomas Children's Laugharne
15. New York Greenwich Village

Introduction by Hannah Ellis

"When did you first become aware that Dylan Thomas was your grandfather?" the intrepid journalist asked, not realising I had been asked the same question many times before. It was very easy to answer. "I've always been aware of him," I confidently replied. "There were paintings and photos of him on my parents' living room wall, poetry books on the shelves translated into various languages and his name was ever-present in everyday discussions." "He is still there," I continued, "in my snub nose and rebellious curly hair and I can see it in my son as he is learning to read, playing with words using a natural and innate gift."

Though I have always been conscious of Dylan Thomas, in the last few years I reluctantly admitted that I took his presence for granted. As an adult, I now understand how privileged I am to be related to such a talented wordsmith and to have been given the wonderful opportunity to regularly visit the beautiful places and communities that were instrumental in developing him as a writer, and as a person.

I feel a strong connection to Wales because of my own childhood memories. It was quite normal at the start of each school holiday to be bundled into a car, soon to be stuck in traffic on the M4, followed by the inevitable bout of carsickness and vomiting across the seats, and then finally asking the typical question "Are we nearly there yet?" The destination, more often than not, was Swansea or Laugharne.

I remember one particular year staying at 5 Cwmdonkin Drive, my grandfather's childhood home. I spent my days that summer roaming about Cwmdonkin Park or exploring the different beaches in the Gower Peninsula, where we jumped the waves in the sea, braving all sorts of weather and never feeling the cold.

I recall another time having a smug 'cut above the rest' attitude as my brother and I ran along the balcony of the Boathouse in Laugharne, ignoring the 'Do not enter' sign, believing the house belonged to us. We also managed to wade into the estuary, fully clothed, getting soaking wet just before the long car journey home.

I share other connections with my grandfather's places, having grown up in London and studied and trained as a teacher in Oxford, the place I made my home for 15 years. I identify with Dylan's desire to want to be part of the 'buzz' and thrilling atmosphere of these two cities, and to absorb the activities of these diverse and cultural hubs. When I went to Greenwich Village in New York, there was a similar electrifying mood. For a young, aspiring writer, the chance to network with fellow poets and artists, along with sharing creative ideas surely must have helped him perfect his craft.

Recently, through my research, I have learnt about the importance of Carmarthenshire and Ceredigion on my grandfather's life and work. The essays and literary tours in this book have further confirmed my belief that the influence of these Welsh-speaking communities is one that is often underestimated.

The Llansteffan Peninsula in Carmarthenshire is the area where Dylan spent all of his childhood holidays, and continued to visit throughout his life. It is a vital place in understanding the impact of Welsh culture and language on his writing. Through hearing the preacher's impassioned sermons in the chapels, he adopted his own unique style when performing his poetry and the equally passionate Sunday school teachers helped him cultivate the art of storytelling. T. James Jones continually surprises me by finding more examples of *cynghanedd* (the Welsh rhyming pattern) in my grandfather's work. It seems to me that Dylan is cleverly weaving two languages together.

The county of Ceredigion was home to my grandparents in the early 1940s. Within months of arriving in New Quay, my grandfather had written a radio script about the small, picturesque sea town called 'Quite Early One Morning', which has many early versions of characters that appear in his later play-for-voices, *Under Milk Wood*. In George Tremlett's essay about the Aeron Valley, he starts by saying "Legend has it that Dylan Thomas' only daughter, Aeronwy, was conceived on the banks of the River Aeron, but she did not believe it and neither did her mother." Whether she was (or was not) conceived there is questionable, but what is clearly true is how deeply affected my grandfather was by the beauty of the area. When abroad, he nostalgically attempts to visualise home. "What birds sounded like and said in Gower; what sort of a sound and a shape was Carmarthen Bay; what silence when night fell in the Aeron Valley."

What I really hope from this book is that we can introduce you to my grandfather's places through his words. That you have the chance to encounter the magnificent countryside, coasts and quirky villages where you too can meet the warm and eccentric people who became the characters in his stories. You will be able to fully comprehend why he was most productive when living close to the sea and amongst the local people that fascinated him.

In the busy and bustling cities, you will quickly understand why he felt at home in certain areas as they were the perfect setting for creative imaginations to join forces. While doing this, my wish is that you forget all the contrasting stories you may have heard, and get to know Dylan Thomas once again by visiting these unique places that inspired his beautiful and memorable writing.

Young Dylan with sister
Nancy on Swansea
beach circa 1920.

Dylan's Swansea Uplands:
The Boy and the Young Dog
by Phil Carradice

Think Dylan Thomas and your mind invariably turns to what was the most influential and significant of all locations for him, the Uplands area of Swansea.

This sprawling suburban enclave was crucial to the young Dylan – for his development as a writer and as an individual. It was where he was born and, arguably, with an iron-fast hold upon his imagination, it was a place he never really left.

The haunts of our childhood have a claim – good or bad – on most of us. But with Dylan Thomas that claim was powerful beyond belief, almost pathological in its intensity. Even after he finally became grounded in Laugharne for the last four years of his life, Swansea – and the Uplands in particular – continued to exercise an incredible pull on his imagination.

Dylan's decline, his long slow slide towards the grave, is symbolised by his longing for a lost life, for a long-gone innocence. He mourned for Cwmdonkin Park and the wonder-filled streets of his childhood, for the Uplands Cinema and the warm comfort of Warmley, Dan Jones' house in Eversley Road. Above all he mourned for his home, 5 Cwmdonkin Drive. It was this mourning that fuelled poems like 'The hunchback in the park' and the stories in *Portrait of the Artist as a Young Dog*.

Dylan was, arguably, a child who never grew up, a poetic Peter Pan who was gifted – or cursed; take your pick – with the amorality of all young children. Whatever he wanted he took, that was his right, just as it had been his right to help himself to handfuls of wine gums from Mrs Ferguson's sweet shop in The Grove when he was ten years old. He lied at will, as children will do, and had the uncanny ability to be all things to all people, altering his stance or approach as necessary – again, just like any precocious four or five-year-old.

Much of his outlandish behaviour in later life can be put down to the simple fact that he saw nothing wrong in what he was doing. Emotionally, Dylan

Thomas had never progressed beyond childhood.

Blame is clearly the wrong word, but there is little doubt that much of the responsibility for this emotional stultification rests with his parents. His mother Florence, with her cosseting, her pampering and pandering to virtually all Dylan's desires, created a womb-like security where every wish was catered for, every dream fulfilled. She protected, she embraced, she virtually embalmed him, in a sickly-sweet, cloying embrace. The house in Cwmdonkin Drive was, for Dylan, a solid physical manifestation of his mother's love.

It is natural for any mother to want to protect her children but Florence took it to extremes. As with any spoiled child Dylan took advantage. He played on his mother's fears, the often repeated story of him cutting his knee with a penknife then telling Florence the blood had come from his ears is just one example of the lengths to which he would go to get that extra ounce of fussing and spoiling.

His father DJ, on the other hand, was a much more formidable character but he too, in his own way, spoiled Dylan. With his books and cultural ideology, with his desire to see his son achieve the success as a writer that had eluded him, DJ imbued Dylan

8758 CWMDONKYN PARK, SWANS[E]

Above: Cwmdonkin Park from a vintage postcard.

Right: 5 Cwmdonkin Drive, Dylan Thomas' birth place.

with a single-mindedness that drove the young man to write and publish. It also added to Dylan's belief that he could do what he liked, whenever he liked.

Dylan's was a small, enclosed world, at least until he went to Swansea Grammar School at the age of 11. It was, at most, a mile wide, from the town centre to the outer reaches of the Uplands and Sketty, from Cwmdonkin Drive southwards to the beach and sea. He might venture out of this enclave but, initially, such trips were in the safety and company of Florence and, later, surrounded by his carefully chosen group of friends. They were merely an extension of his known world.

The very smallness of this world meant safety and security. It was familiar, it was comforting; as reassuring as Mam's hugs and sickbed mothering. But within that Uplands security Dylan could reign supreme.

He was the king of Cwmdonkin Park, lord of the back seats in the flea-pit Uplands Cinema – his was the right to steal sweets and cigarettes from Mrs Ferguson, to knock on doors and run. Even at Mrs Hole's Dame School in Mirador Crescent, where he received his first formal education, he held the position of honour on the lap of Mrs Hole's daughter – more cosseting, this time from a mother surrogate, albeit for a short time but infinitely

THE SONG OF THE MISCHIEVOUS DOG.

There are many who say that a dog has its day,
   And a cat has a number of lives ;
There are others who think that a lobster is pink,
   And that bees never work in their hives.
There are fewer, of course, who insist that a horse
   Has a horn and two humps on its head,
And a fellow who jests that a mare can build nests
   Is as rare as a donkey that's red.
Yet in spite of all this, I have moments of bliss,
   For I cherish a passion for bones,
And though doubtful of biscuit, I'm willing to risk it,
   And love to chase rabbits and stones.
But my greatest delight is to take a good bite
   At a calf that is plump and delicious ;
And if I indulge in a bite at a bulge,
   Let's hope you won't think me too vicious.

D. M. THOMAS 3A.

Oh as I was young and easy in the mercy of his means
time held me green and dying
though I sang in my chains like the sea

DYLAN THOMAS

preferable to the rigours of maths and music.

These Uplands days were a paradise – small wonder he spent the rest of his life trying to get back there. Even in adolescence the Uplands continued to provide security. A brief period as a reporter on the local paper was followed by three years in the safety and security of his room in 5 Cwmdonkin Drive, a tiny sanctuary but one that was familiar enough to allow him to express himself in a monumental welter of poems.

The Uplands Hotel was his first 'drinking hole', although it was also his father's bolt hole and could, therefore, be used only sparingly.

But there were still friends like composer Daniel Jones, painter Alfred Janes and communist grocer Bert Trick to meet and talk with.

It is almost impossible to stress the significance of the Uplands on Dylan Thomas as a writer. It is a misnomer to say that he left Swansea to go to London – he did not really leave. A fortnight, three weeks, away from Mam and Cwmdonkin Drive was about all he could manage before he fled back to suburban Swansea, a whole world away from his supposed bohemian longings. And back in the Uplands the spoiling and the fussing started again.

Dylan at Blaen Cwm.

South Carmarthenshire:
The Sound and Shape of Carmarthen Bay
by Gillian Clarke

LITERARY · · TOUR MAP 2

...And as I was green and carefree, famous among the barns About the happy yard and Singing as the farm was home...

Auntie Annie & Uncle Jim lived at fernhill farm

The farms of Dylan's family

Pen y coed

Waun fwlchan

the CLIP-CLOP Cynghanedd of a horse's hooves

Capel newydd

Llanybri

Lon y Deri

Old School Road

visits to Lynette Roberts & Keidrych Rhys at Tŷ Gwyn

Dylan's FAVOURITE PUB: the Edwinsford Arms run by his relatives Thomas & Catherine

LLANSTEFFAN

LAUGHARNE

High Street

Fernhill FARM

Llangain →

Blaen Cwm

312

River Towy

Three months before the hundredth birthday of Dylan Thomas, a Belgian Ardennes mare called Leila leaned into her harness and pulled a covered wagon weighed with passengers and driver through sunlit Carmarthenshire lanes, on pilgrimage to Fernhill, Waunfwlchan, Blaen Cwm, Llanybri, Laugharne; places redolent with the poet's work.

In places thorny wands lashed the wagon's open sides, "twisting out to twig the mare by the bridle and poke our caps".[1] On steep hills we alighted, to help Leila, sweating in the heat, her hooves slipping on the steep track. On level ground she clopped easily, her beautiful rump like a glossy giant peach before us.

Her hoof-beats rhymed the day. Horses – with owls, cockerels, and herons – are Dylan's beasts of yard and field, as china dogs and stuffed foxes are his parlour creatures. The poet's work is full of horses, and carts, "Heigh, on horseback hill"[2], and "honoured among wagons" where he heard "blessed among stables ... the horses /Flashing into the dark", and "the spellbound horses walking warm /Out of the whinnying green stable/On to the fields of praise."[3]

Hoof-beats were the iambics of the place. The pentameter of "do not go gentle into that good night"[4], echoing the rhythm of horse and cart on a country lane, was familiar to schoolboy Dylan, riding beside inebriated Uncle Jim home to Fernhill, "the lilting house" where he was "young and easy", and where, spooked by the dark yard, he bolted into Auntie Annie's arms. Uncle Jim, Fernhill's tenant farmer, stole piglets from the sow to pay for his pleasures in favourite watering haunts

Above: Fernhill Farm.

Right: Capel Newydd Llanybri.

The Hare's Foot, or The Pure Drop, after market day in Carmarthen, as described in Dylan's story 'The Peaches'. The house, Gorsehill in the story, "where the cobbles rang and the black empty stables took up the ringing ... the hollow house at the end of the yard", where "every stair had a different voice", is a faded Georgian house behind padlocked gates. I had imagined a traditional stone farmhouse, not this tired grandeur, but a place "green and golden", where "all the sun long it was running, it was lovely".[5]

Dylan's parents' roots were in rural Carmarthenshire, as were those of my own paternal family. His family, like mine, were mostly respectable, chapel-going, Welsh-speaking, 'tidy' working-class. Such people minded about a well-scrubbed doorstep, Chapel on Sundays, a cooked dinner, a clean cloth on the table. Welsh was the family language, until Dylan's father chose English, and elocution lessons, for his son. When Dylan's parents moved up a notch into Swansea's suburbia, the farmhouse objects, "the knitted text, 'Prepare to Meet thy God', ... the grandmother clock, the smiling china dogs," survived as relics. In Dylan's 1930-32 notebook is a little note of desperation, scrawled in his box bedroom at 5 Cwmdonkin Drive:

On the gravestone:
ER COF ANNWYL AM

MOUNT PLEASANT LLANGAIN
HUNODD CHWEF 7, 1933, YN 70 OED.

HUNODD MEDI 3, 1942, YN 76 OED.

Top left: Family photo, circa 1909. Back row standing: Arthur (D. J.'s brother, Dylan's uncle), another brother Tom and his wife, Florence and D. J. (Dylan's parents). Front row, seated: Evan, Dylan's sister Nancy on Anne's knee (Evan and Anne, Dylan's grandparents).

Bottom left: Dylan's parents.

Above: Ann Jones' grave.

"(Oh change the life!),/The sideboard fruit, the ferns, the picture houses/And the pack of cards."

A sideboard had replaced the dresser, a pack of cards the knitted text. Much later, in London, he describes how, when not in Wales, he easily remembered the superficial things, "settles in the corners, hams on the hooks", but found it "harder to remember what birds sounded like and said in Gower, what sort of a sound and shape was Carmarthen Bay".

Dylan heard Welsh spoken at Fernhill, sung in Smyrna chapel, recited at *Eisteddfodau*. It is the tongue of "the lilting house", and "the barns about the happy yard". The rhythm of a horse's hooves heard in his childhood echoes again in his lament for his dying father. He writes of time as if then and now, a radiant past and a grieving present were one, lost joy recalled, the more luminous for death's shadow. Dylan's greatest poems are both "green and dying", at once lit by childhood joy and darkened by its loss.

In the sunlit lane at Fernhill we heard what he heard – the lane where "time" let the poet-child hail the horse-drawn wagon to stop for him to climb the "house-high hay" and ride home, "prince of the apple towns". We heard, too, from the other Fernhill, Gorsehill

From
IN MEMORY
OF ANN JONES

AFTER the feast of tear-stuffed time and thistles
In a room with a stuffed fox and a stale fern,
I stand, for this memorial's sake, alone
In the snivelling hours with dead, humped Ann
Whose hooded, fountain heart once fell in puddles
Round the parched world of Wales and drowned each sun
[Though this for her is a monstrous image blindly
Magnified out of praise ; her death was a still drop ;
She would not have me sinking in the holy
Flood of her heart's fame ; she would lie dumb and deep
And need no druid of her broken body].
But I, Ann's bard on a raised hearth, call all
The seas to service that her wood-tongued virtue
Babble like a bellbuoy over the hymning heads,
Bow down the walls of the ferned and foxy woods
That her love ring and swing through a brown chapel,
Bless her bent spirit with four, crossing birds.
Her flesh was meek as milk, but this skyward statue
With the wild breast and blessed and giant skull
Is carved from her in a room with a wet window
In a fiercely mourning house in a crooked year.
I know her scrubbed and sour humble hands
Lie with religion in their cramp, her threadbare
Whisper in a damp word, her wits drilled hollow,
Her fist of a face died clenched on a round pain ;
And sculptured Ann is seventy years of stone.
These cloud-sopped, marble hands, this monumental
Argument of the hewn voice, gesture and psalm
Storm me forever over her grave until
The stuffed lung of the fox twitch and cry Love
And the strutting fern lay seeds on the black sill.

DYLAN THOMAS

Drawing by Brenda Chamberlain

Left: The 1942 Caseg Press printing of *After the Funeral* with Brenda Chamberlain's haunting illustration.

of 'The Peaches', the ring of cobbles, how "the black empty stables took up the ringing and hollowed it", and "the different voice of every stair."

On through "the parables of sunlight" of his far away childhood and our present, past Waunfwlchan, Blaen Cwm, leaving Leila and the trap for the bus to Penycoed, the churchyard at Llanybri, Ann Jones' grave, to Laugharne and Brown's Hotel, and the Boathouse on its "breakneck of rocks", where waves are horses:

"With wild sea fillies and soaking bridles/With salty colts and gales in their limbs/All the horses of his haul of miracles/Gallop through the arched, green farms" [6]

Dylan Thomas had perfect pitch for the music of being human, and the rhythms of Welsh, that other drum, retune his English for a new poetry.

This music, this truth, voices the very "sound and shape of Carmarthen Bay", and the place speaks it still: the tidy wives, the mussel-pickers, the heron-priested shore. 'Fern Hill' sings

aloud his unique genius. His obsession with "time" brings the sensuous, sunlit dream-world of childhood into the darkness of now and turns it to song, and the poem's closing lines psalm the shape and sound of life and death:

"Time held me green and dying/ Though I sang in my chains like the sea".

[1] 'The Peaches'

[2] 'Prologue' to *Collected Poems*

[3] 'Fern Hill'

[4] 'Do not go gentle into that goodnight'

[5] 'Fern Hill'

[6] 'Ballad of the Long-legged Bait'

Dylan Thomas echoes
James Dean.

Swansea Hollywood:
The Mummy and the Old Dark House
by Berwyn Rowlands

LITERARY
· 3 ·
TOUR MAP

SWANSEA HOLLYWOOD

Volcano THEATRE

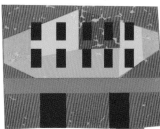

HIGH street

Uplands Cinema

the Kingsway

Elysium Gallery

CASTLE Street

worcester place

CARLTON Cinema

castle Square

CAER

Wind str

OXFORD street

Salubrious PLACE →

singleton street

SWANSEA GRAND theatre

Princess way

Palace Theatre

Castle Cinema

Strand

Oystermouth Road

We know that Dylan Thomas was an avid film fan but he can also be described as a film buff when we read the pretentious but informed article he wrote for his school magazine in 1930 at the age of just 15.

Wales' greatest poet, writing in English, also scripted many feature films, contributed to the war effort with propaganda films and featured as the leading man in biopic after biopic many years after his death. But what did he see in Swansea in those early years which would find him contributing to the world of film-making?

Everybody in 1930s and 1940s Britain was a film fan. By the end of the 1930s, cinema was the most important form of mass entertainment in the western world. One billion tickets were sold in the UK alone in 1939, a country with a population of about 47 million. During this decade, three cinemas a week were opening in the UK. Dylan Thomas probably contributed to these sales figures.

Swansea was not unusual in the number of cinemas serving the area. Wales' second largest city could boast cinemas not just in the city centre but also dotted around the suburbs including Uplands, Manselton, Sketty and Townhill. It is quite certain that Dylan Thomas would have been able to see films in Swansea in more than one cinema.

On the corner of High Street and Bethesda Street, a stone's throw from the railway station, stands the Palace Theatre. Today the building is a depressing example of historical vandalism camouflaged in green foliage. Although originally built as a Music Hall in 1888, it also showed one of the earliest silent film screenings in Wales.

The Elysium, further down the High Street, is also challenging to look at today without feeling a sense of loss, as it is in such a bad state of repair that I wouldn't even venture inside with a hard hat today. The Castle Cinema on Worcester Place is in a better state, but converted into something called LaserZone.

Above and right:
The Old Carlton Cinema – now Waterstones bookshop.

For 63 years, The Carlton Cine De Lux screened major movies for the cinema-loving people of Swansea, including, we assume, Dylan Thomas. The interior has been stunningly preserved and the listed front of house foyer and café is now open for the public to enjoy. The auditorium, alas, is no more; Waterstones had to put the books somewhere, which I guess would have pleased Dylan Thomas.

These buildings survived the Blitz undamaged as much of Swansea city centre, including Dylan's beloved Kardomah Café, was destroyed by the German bombers during the Second World War.

What kind of films would Dylan Thomas have seen in Swansea? There were plenty of cinemas, but in reality how much choice would there have been in Swansea during the 30s and 40s?

British cinema was in a state of decline by the end of the 1920s. When the Carlton Cine De Lux opened in 1914 about a quarter of films available to the public would have been British. This fell to 5% with the rise in popularity of Hollywood produced films – some things never change.

About a third of the British population would have seen *Snow White and the Seven Dwarfs* in 1937. Other memorable titles would include Victor Fleming's popular crowd pleasers *The Wizard of Oz* and *Gone with the*

Above: The Palace Theatre.

Right: One of Dylan's favourite fleapit cinemas. It was next door to the Evening Post offices where he worked.

Below right: Young Dylan Thomas writes on film in the Swansea Grammar School Magazine July 1930 (he was aged 15).

Battleship Potemkin (1925). It is not certain whether these films would have been available in the Swansea cinemas, but he would have been able to see them on his travels.

Dylan Thomas wrote confidently as a 15-year-old boy about the evolution of the motion picture, starting with D. W. Griffith and concluding with the introduction of sound and synchronized films, in an article for the Swansea Grammar School Magazine in July 1930. Interestingly he confirms, without referencing many titles, the dominance of American producers in British cinemas, especially after the suspension of film-making in England during the War. He concludes however, "the pictures produced in this country are quite as good and nearly as many as those produced in America."

The destruction of much of Swansea during the Blitz, on reflection, had more of a direct influence on Dylan Thomas becoming a scriptwriter than any film he might have seen in his beloved city. Unable to join some of his friends fighting for King and Country due to his ill health, Dylan moved to

Wind, both released in 1939. Earlier that decade you would probably have seen *The 39 Steps* directed by Alfred Hitchcock (1935) and *Modern Times* staring and directed by Charlie Chaplin (1936).

Like most of Swansea, Dylan Thomas would have seen the popular films. We know that he also liked and watched many of the classics including

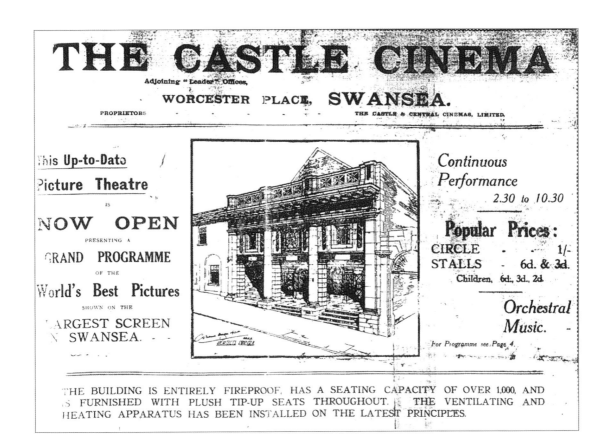

THE CASTLE CINEMA

Adjoining " Leader " Offices,

WORCESTER PLACE, SWANSEA.

PROPRIETORS · · · THE CASTLE & CENTRAL CINEMAS, LIMITED.

This Up-to-Date
Picture Theatre
IS
NOW OPEN
PRESENTING A
GRAND PROGRAMME
OF THE
World's Best Pictures
SHOWN ON THE
LARGEST SCREEN
IN SWANSEA. - -

*Continuous
Performance*
2.30 to 10.30

Popular Prices:
CIRCLE · · 1/-
STALLS · 6d. & 3d.
Children, 6d., 3d., 2d.

*Orchestral
Music.*

For Programme see Page 4.

THE BUILDING IS ENTIRELY FIREPROOF, HAS A SEATING CAPACITY OF OVER 1,000, AND IS FURNISHED WITH PLUSH TIP-UP SEATS THROUGHOUT. THE VENTILATING AND HEATING APPARATUS HAS BEEN INSTALLED ON THE LATEST PRINCIPLES.

◇ ◇ ◇

THE FILMS.

The evolution of the motion-picture from the crude experimentalism of pre-war years to the polished artistry of to-day has taken place during a very short period. It was not until the beginning of the twentieth century that it was possible to present natural things in natural motion on a screen. To-day, less than thirty years later, every shade of physical emotion, however slight or subtle, can be shown among natural and often naturally coloured surroundings.

The first picture that *could* be taken seriously was produced by D. W. Griffith in 1907. He brought a greater sense of balance and artistic understanding to that film than had hitherto been thought of, and introduced the now familiar tricks of the " close-up," the " fade out " and the " cut back." He realised the importance of motion-pictures, not as freak exhibitions, but as works of art produced through an entirely new medium. The first film that *was* taken seriously was Adolph Zukar's " Queen Elizabeth," produced in 1912. Zukar had been for a long time contemplating the introduction of famous stage-stars on to the screen, and he made his first attempt at this by casting Sara Bernhardt as Elizabeth. The film met with instant appreciation, but, with a few notable exceptions, stage-stars have not been successful on the screen,

Above: Dylan, Griffith Williams and Spanish actor Mario Cabré on the Pendine beach film location for *Pandora and the Flying Dutchman*.

Right: Cinema fare at the Mumbles.

THE NEW CINEMA NEWTON ROAD, MUMBLES.

Continuous 6.30 to 10.   Matinee Saturdays 2.30.   Telephone: Mumbles 456.

SPECIAL HOLIDAY ATTRACTIONS.

Programme for Week Commencing, December 24th, Monday, Tuesday, Wednesday.
PAULINE FREDERICK in the Greatest "Mother-Love" Role

"MUMSIE."

LILIAN HALL DAVIES in a masterly Adaption of "King's Mate" the Famous novel.
"THE WHITE SHIEK."

Thursday, Friday, Saturday.
FAY COMPTON as ROSALIND NIGHTINGALE in
"SOMEHOW GOOD."
REGINAL DENNY in "THE NIGHT BIRD."

Week Commencing December 31st, Monday, Tuesday, Wednesday,
Ellaline Terriss in "LAND of HOPE and GLORY."
BEBE DANIELS in "SHE'S A SHIEK."

Thursday, Friday, Saturday,
John Barrymore in "THE BELOVED ROGUE."
George Jessel and Warner Oland in "Sailor Izzy Murphy."

POETRY AND FILM

London shortly after the infamous bombing raids of February 1941. He was initially ignored by the Ministry of Information (MOI) but by a quirk of fate found employment with the Strand Film Group, who in turn were producing films for the MOI. Dylan was quite prolific at this time, writing at least five films in 1942.

After the war he went on to write film scripts for Gainsborough and in 1951 he even travelled to Iran to write a script, which was never filmed, for the Anglo-Iranian Oil Company.

It is worth noting that his script *The Doctor and The Devils* was the first to be published but was not made into a film until 1985. Welsh greats Timothy Dalton and Jonathan Pryce would star, maintaining a link with Wales.

One can only imagine how many films we did not get to see thanks to the untimely death of Dylan Thomas. How many would have made it back to the cinemas of Swansea, we will never know.

Above: One of Dylan's last public appearances in New York with Arthur Miller.

GOWER

DYLAN THOMAS   By AUGUSTUS JOHN

VOLUME SIX

Three Shillings

Cover of the 1954 memorial
issue of *Gower*, the Gower
Society's Journal.

Gower and Mumbles:
The Townie, the Actor and the Comedian
by Jeff Towns

Swansea

Castle Square

CASTLE St

offices of
THE DAILY POST

PRINCESS WAY

salubrious
PLACE

DYLAN invoked spirits before a PLAY

ARTHUR'S STONE
Cefn Bryn

the LOCALS:

Dan Jones

Colleagues from
The Daily Post

Vernon Watkins

Bert TRICK

the socialist grocer

the Village Inn

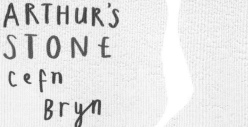

Three Cliffs BAY

residence of Vernon Watkins

HEATHERSLADE

MUMBLES

The Antelope

kardomah cafe

WIND St

oystermouth

Swansea Little THEATRE

Mumbles Rd

Dylan Thomas always saw himself as an urban creature, a lover of the town and the city; of smoky interiors rather than wide open spaces; of busy roads rather than country lanes.

He told his closest poetic friend, Vernon Watkins, who lived on Gower:

"I am not a countryman; I stand for the provincial drive, the morning café, the evening pub."

Dylan was born in a Swansea suburb but the nearby Gower Peninsula was an area rich in natural beauty and rugged coastal scenery and, in 1956, it was officially designated as the first 'Area of Outstanding Natural Beauty' in the UK. In his youth this area was crucial to Dylan's development and during schoolboy summers he camped there, often for weeks at a time. He enjoyed, and would sing the praises of Gower. In 1933 he began his epistolary courtship of Pamela Hansford Johnson, who he met through the poetry column of *The Sunday Referee* newspaper.

In an early 1934 letter he writes:

"Gower is a very beautiful peninsula, some miles from the blowsy town and so far the tea-shop philistines have not spoilt the more beautiful of its bays ... Gower as a matter of fact is one of the loveliest sea-coast stretches in the whole of Britain and some of its villages are as obscure, as little inhabited and as lovely as they were a hundred years ago."

At this point in the letter Dylan inserted a note in the margin which says "this sounds like a passage from a tourist guide". The letter continues:

"One day when I know you even better than I do now, you must come down and stay with me. Swansea is a dingy hell, and my mother is a vulgar humbug, but I am not so bad and Gower is as beautiful as anywhere."

And, perhaps in an effort to make himself sound romantic and interesting, he describes to her how he loves, "walking alone over the very desolate Gower cliffs, communing with the cold and quietness."

Above: Pamela Hansford Johnson; Dylan and Pamela Hansford Johnson at Caswell.

Right: Mumbles Village.

Pamela did eventually come to Swansea and she and her mother stayed in The Mermaid in Mumbles, one of Dylan's favourite watering holes, but the furthest Dylan took her into Gower was Caswell Bay. A grainy photograph survives of the two of them canoodling on the beach in which Dylan is seen practising that peculiar Welsh skill of kissing whilst still having a cigarette stuck firmly to his lower lip.

As a young boy Dylan was often taken to the Gower village of Newton, which is up above Mumbles, to visit his aunt Dosie, his mother's sister. She had married a minister – the Reverend David Rees. He was the minister at Paraclete Congregational Church and the couple lived in the adjoining Manse. Although not too happy about having to attend up to three church services on his regular Sunday visits, it was here that Dylan obtained his deep knowledge of the Bible that infuses his work. Also he absorbed his uncle's preaching style, laced with hell-fire and brimstone and delivered in a booming voice steeped in Welsh *hwyl*, which Dylan would utilise in his future radio and public poetry performances. As Dylan himself commented:

"The great rhythms had rolled over me from Welsh pulpits and I had read for myself from Job to Ecclesiastes; and

THE
OLD
MANSE
✝
"NOW AS I WAS YOUNG
AND EASY·UNDER THE APPLE
BOUGHS·ABOUT THE LILTING
HOUSE·AND HAPPY AS THE
··GRASS WAS GREEN"
DYLAN THOMAS
STAYED HERE

Vernon Watkins by Alfred Jones 1947, City & County

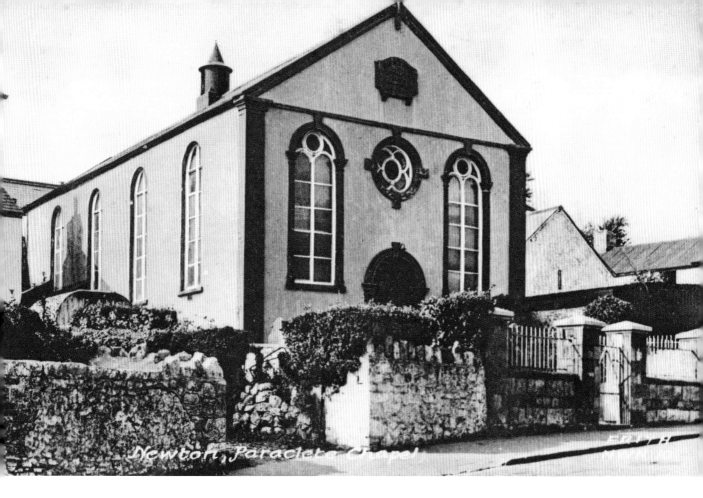

Newton, Paraclete Chapel

the story of the New Testament is a part of my life."

It was the Rev. Rees who put the poet Vernon Watkins in touch with Dylan in 1934. As their friendship developed, Dylan would often visit Vernon at his home on the cliffs at Pennard. Vernon would drag a reluctant Dylan along for cliff walks and beach rambles, but could not get Dylan to join him in his regular swims in the clear waters of Hunt's Cove.

As a young actor with Swansea's Little Theatre, Dylan toured in productions up into the South Wales Valleys and out across Gower. On one tour to Reynoldston on Gower, the cast stopped for a late night refreshment at the King Arthur pub, whereupon Dylan led them all on an eerie walk up to Arthur's Stone on top of Cefn Bryn. One of his co-actresses, Evelyn Burman, recalled how he proceeded to:

"... lead us round the stone, chanting all the time, making up a spell that included juice from wortle-berry, slime from a snail and other repulsive articles. His acting was so convincing that I nearly passed out with fright!"

Despite his 'townie' protestations two of his finest autobiographical short stories are set at the very tip of Gower. Published in 1940, *Portrait of the Artist as a Young Dog* comprises of ten stories that give us a very lightly

Above: Rhossili Bay,
Gower Peninsula;
Arthur's Stone,
Cefn Bryn.

fictionalised account of the writer's early life. Of these, two are set in rural Carmarthenshire, six in urban and suburban Swansea town, but two, 'Extraordinary Little Cough' and 'Who Do you Wish Was With Us' are set in Rhossili, a small idyllic village on the south-western tip of the Gower Peninsula. 'Extraordinary Little Cough' tells of a camping adventure enjoyed by Dylan and his friends as young teens, and involves girls, bullying and long distance running. 'Who Do You Wish Was With Us' is a more poignant story involving Dylan's friend Trevor Hughes, who has just lost members of his family to tuberculosis. Together they embark on a long hike down to the atmospheric outcrop of rock – the

Above: The Worm's Head Hotel, Rhossili Bay, Gower.

Worm's Head, that dominates the view from Rhossili. Dylan looks out across the ocean towards America and declares:

"Instead of becoming small on the great rock poised between sky and sea, I felt myself the size of a breathing building ... as I said: 'Why don't we live here always? Always and always. Build a bloody house and live like bloody kings!'"

Towards the end of his life, Dylan's old school friend Guido Heller took over the hotel at Rhossili and Dylan and Caitlin paid him a visit. On spotting the isolated Old Rectory down on the downs, Dylan decided he had had enough of Laugharne and that this romantic Gower mansion was more to his liking, announcing his desire to move there forthwith. However, when Guido pointed out to him that his hotel was unlicensed and that the nearest pub was a good few miles away, Dylan quickly changed his mind.

A young Dylan, aged 19.

Welsh Language in the Work of Dylan Thomas
by T. James Jones

Dan y Coed Halt

Llwyfan Cerrig

the rhythm of train wheels as they move over the tracks......

B4301

to New Quay and the Aeron Valley

Gwili RAILWAY

River Gwili

A484

Dylan Thomas used the poetic form of CYNGHANEDD in 'Fern Hill'

Welsh was more widely spoken here than in Swansea

BRONWYDD ARMS

to Carmarthen and Llangain

When the schoolboy Dylan went on summer holidays to Fernhill farm near Llangain, he would have gone by train from Swansea to Carmarthen.

But later Dylan frequently visited Ceredigion, staying in various places near Lampeter and Aberaeron and living for nine months in 1944 at New Quay, during which time he began writing *Under Milk Wood*. Consequently he would have used the Carmarthen to Aberystwyth railway line. The Gwili Railway is a Welsh heritage railway line on the former Carmarthen to Aberystwyth railway that closed in 1965. Originally it was a line from Carmarthen to Newcastle Emlyn with a junction at Pencader enabling a through route to Llandysul, Lampeter and Aberystwyth.

Dylan was given his middle name, Marlais, in order to preserve the memory of his great uncle Gwilym Marles, a Unitarian minister of religion who led the radical political protests against the oppression of the landlords in nineteenth century Wales. By giving his son this middle name, his father, D. J. Thomas, seemingly wished to preserve and connect with the radical tradition engendered by Gwilym Marles, an accomplished Welsh-language poet who also established a grammar school in Llandysul.

When the schoolboy Dylan travelled on the train as far as Carmarthen to spend his summer holidays on his aunt Annie's farm, Fernhill, in the village of Llangain a few miles from Carmarthen, his journey would have taken him from a predominantly English-language environment in suburban Swansea to the rural districts of west Carmarthenshire. Here, as in the neighbouring county of Ceredigion, Welsh would have been the dominant language of the agricultural community and of the nonconformist religion such as that of Smyrna Chapel at Llangain which Annie frequented thrice on a Sunday.

In those chapel services Dylan would have heard preachers conveying the Gospel message in the unique

Above: Capel Smyrna Llangain.

Right: Dylan's great uncle Gwilym Marles.

Welsh mode of what was known as *hwyl*, which was characterised by a musical intonation or cadence used in the ecstatic climax in the peroration of the sermon. In his short story 'The Peaches' he reproduces this in Gwilym's sermon in his 'chapel' in the Fernhill barn. He hears Gwilym's voice "rise and crack and sink to a whisper and break into singing and Welsh and ring triumphantly ... " The peroration famously reaches its climax by comparing the Divine Being's visual ability with that of a feline: "Thou canst see all the time, O God, mun, you're like a bloody cat."

Traces of *hwyl* could be detected in the unique style of Dylan's delivery of his poems. In 'After the Funeral' he adopted the Welsh traditional role of being a praise poet. He named himself "Ann's bard" reflecting the exaggerated eulogies composed by the traditional Welsh poet-preacher.

The style of Dylan's prose, his essays and pieces for radio and short stories would also have been influenced by the New Testament parables related by experienced Sunday school teachers such as those of Smyrna Chapel. And Dylan's art of storytelling would have been nurtured by his

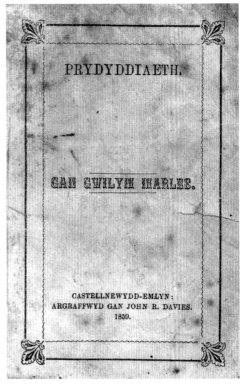

listening to natural exponents of this art on the hearths of the farmsteads he visited on his school holidays, before the advent of an alternative entertainment which was soon to be provided by television. Dylan was to reach the zenith of the Welsh art of storytelling when he himself adopted the role of the *cyfarwydd* (storyteller) at the Poetry Center in New York in his performance as First Voice in the first public reading of *Under Milk Wood* on 14 May 1953.

Dylan's school day railway journeys westward took him from childhood to adolescence. In the poem 'Fern Hill' he remembered how he suddenly became aware of time transforming the place that had made him "happy as the grass was green" into a "childless land". Those days marked the end of his childhood, an important part of which had been spent in Welsh Wales. The closing three lines of 'Fern Hill' reflect this in an artistically subtle way, since two of the final three lines are in the unique Welsh thousand-year-old art form of *cynghanedd:*

"Oh as I was young and easy in the mercy of his means,/Time held me green and dying/Though I sang in my chains like the sea."

In the first of these lines Dylan chose to use his favourite form of *cynghanedd* – which is called *cynghanedd sain* (his poetry contains very many such lines; my favourite being "Though the town below lay leaved with October blood" – 'Poem in October'.)

In the above line from 'Fern Hill' *cynghanedd sain* uses internal rhymes – 'easy/mercy' as well as a consonantal reflection – 'mercy/means'. Although the penultimate line does not contain *cynghanedd* the internal rhyme in 'dying' is reflected by the word 'my' in the final line, a device often used by *cynghanedd* poets.

The final line is another form of *cynghanedd* – *cynghanedd draws* – whereby the opening consonants 'th' and 's' in "Though I sang" are reflected in "the sea". Incidentally, this line provides an excellent definition of this art form, since the poet who writes in *cynghanedd* is singing within certain rules or "chains" of harmony, or to use a more appropriate metaphor in the context of these thoughts, like the wheels of a train moving rhythmically along their tracks.

Ceri Richards lithograph
The Force 1945.

The force that through the green fuse drives the flowe
Drives my green age ;

Dylan Thomas and Organic Surrealism
by Pascale Petit

Dylan Thomas wrote 'The force that through the green fuse drives the flower' before he was 19.

Although he would later reject the movement's label, this poem reveals a deep symbolist surrealism working on an organic level. A green fuse electrifies all nature in a shamanistic image that has the atavistic power of Arthur Rimbaud's *Les Illuminations*. Thomas even referred to himself as "the Rimbaud of Cwmdonkin Drive". He has the incantatory vigour of the French symbolist and he embraced Rimbaud's credo of a systematic derangement of all the senses, both in the trance of his lines and in the drinking excesses of his life. His poems are not random automatic jottings though; there is too much depth, a meticulous crafting which gives the lines their sculpted feel.

This organic surrealism influenced me both as a visual artist and poet. So much so that in 1990 when London Underground commissioned me to paint a poster for the Tube I titled it 'The Force that Through the Green Fuse'. Central to my composition is Thomas' life force driving all matter:

"The force that through the green fuse drives the flower/Drives my green age; that blasts the roots of trees/ Is my destroyer."

My poster commemorated the reopening of the refurbished Palm House at Kew Gardens. This greenhouse contains the first oxygen-makers of our planet – prehistoric cycads. In my painting these cycads are spark plugs or fuse wires that set the whole eco-system alight. I saw the Palm House as a botanical zoo where the last rainforests of the earth are preserved, kept under glass domes like patients in intensive care. Yet these endangered plants also suggest nuclear energy.

Surrealism is a broad movement, veering from the profound to nonsense.

FIVE

THE force that through the green fuse drives the flower
  Drives my green age ; that blasts the roots of trees
Is my destroyer.
And I am dumb to tell the crooked rose
My youth is bent by the same wintry fever.

The force that drives the water through the rocks
Drives my red blood ; that dries the mouthing streams
Turns mine to wax.
And I am dumb to mouth unto my veins
How at the mountain spring the same mouth sucks.

The hand that whirls the water in the pool
Stirs the quicksand ; that ropes the blowing wind
Hauls my shroud sail.
And I am dumb to tell the hanging man
How of my clay is made the hangman's lime.

The lips of time leech to the fountain head ;
Love drips and gathers, but the fallen blood
Shall calm her sores.
And I am dumb to tell a weather's wind
How time has ticked a heaven round the stars.

And I am dumb to tell the lover's tomb
How at my sheet goes the same crooked worm.

17

Above: Dylan's self-portrait; 'The force that through the green fuse drives the flower' first published in *18 Poems* in 1934.

Right: Dylan's self-portrait on the cover of his first book *18 Poems*.

Page 109: Dylan's only known surrealist painting.

At its most frivolous, it can be off-putting – Salvador Dalí walking a giant anteater around the streets of Paris. The Comte de Lautréamont has defined it as being "beautiful as the chance encounter between a sewing machine and an umbrella on an operating table". It has also been defined by André Breton as the unconscious, archetypal myth, the use of chance, the irrational, hidden desires (the taboo or transgressional), and has memorably been described by the poet Luis Aragon as "a wave of dreams". It can also be the uncensored creative impulses of automatic writing.

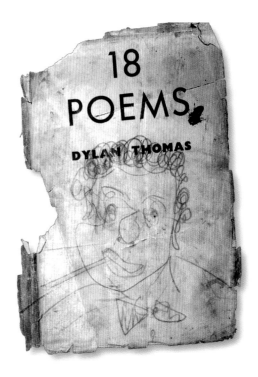

A PETITION TO THE GOVERNMENT

Dylan Thomas

Above: Dylan and Caitlin, Flagstaff, Arizona on their way to stay with Max Ernst.

Right: Max Ernst gave this copy of *Misfortunes of the Immortals* to Dylan and Caitlin.

Although Thomas' poetry seems to come from the subconscious, the organic aspect of his surrealism is anything but whimsical. Yet the movement has been criticised for encouraging his tendency to write obscurely. In his poem 'Altarwise by owl-light' the phantasmagoria of images adds up to a rather inaccessible whole. The idea of automatic writing not needing to make sense could generate obscure poetry, but Thomas' organic surrealism tends towards clarity.

The Welsh painter Ceri Richards engaged with Thomas' surrealism at its deepest level in his series of lithographs that respond to 'The force that through the green fuse drives the flower'. In Richards' semi-abstract jewel-like illustrations, which bear the same titles as lines from the poem, he creates a visual equivalent of Thomas' dualism. The force that drives nature is also the force that "drives my green age" and "is my destroyer". Richards' images are full of burgeoning life but under the soil a skeleton feeds the roots of his flower; life and death are entangled. This is a rooted, chthonic super-realism.

The dissident Chinese poet Yang Lian has defined surrealism as "deep reality" that erupts from the root and is super-real. He wrote:

"Much contemporary Chinese poetry gives western readers the impression of surrealism. But to me, playing such games with images which seem obscure but are actually so simple is a diminishment of real writing. All of my efforts were focused on the depth of reality."

Yang Lian's images are mosaics of strangely juxtaposed objects, but he considers his surrealism to be "deep reality" – imagery with roots, rather than a surrealism that might just be obscure or playful ornament.

I think that's what this poem 'The force that through the green fuse' does,

its reality comes from the marrow, rather than the skin. This root-reality is integral to many elemental surrealists such as Dorothea Tanning, Remedios Varo, Max Ernst and Frida Kahlo. The American painter Dorothea Tanning, in her painting 'Ein Klein Nachtmusik' (1943), is one example. Although she depicts an interior, the forces of nature dominate. Two little girls are blown by an elemental wind like the force through the green fuse, while a giant sunflower menaces them with its solar power.

Some of Dylan Thomas' poems embrace the psychotropic derangements of Rimbaud's 'Une Saison en Enfer' or 'Le Bateau Ivre'. In Thomas' poem 'In Country Sleep' the images are wildly visionary: "Illumination of music! The lulled black-backed / Gull, on the wave with

The force that through the green fuse drives the flower
Drives my green age ; that blasts the roots of trees
Is my destroyer.
And I am dumb to tell the crooked rose
My youth is bent by the same wintry fever.

The force that drives the water through the rocks
Drives my red blood ; that dries the mouthing streams
Turns mine to wax.
And I am dumb to mouth unto my veins
How at the mountain spring the same mouth sucks.

The hand that whirls the water in the pool
Stirs the quicksand ; that ropes the blowing wind
Hauls my shroud sail.
And I am dumb to tell the hanging man
How of my clay is made the hangman's lime.

The lips of time leech to the fountain head
Love drips and gathers, but the fallen blood
Shall calm her sores.
And I am dumb to tell a weather's wind
How time has ticked a heaven round the stars.

And I am dumb to tell the lover's tomb
How at my sheet goes the same crooked worm.

Dylan Thomas

Left: Ceri Richards lithograph 'The force that through the green grass drives the flower' 1945.

Above: *Ancestral Memory* by Pascale Petit, 1984, (9'x5'x3', glass, thorns, birds, insects, clocks, torn photos).

sand in its eyes [...] Earth, air, water, fire, singing into the white act". But even then there is the organic "beat of blood through the laced leaves".

Another of Thomas' well-known poems, 'Fern Hill', culminates in a supremely surreal line: "though I sang in my chains like the sea". Up till then the poem seems un-surreal, more a praise poem or pastoral, a straightforward celebration of Fernhill and youth, but with an elegiac tone. Until we get to that heart-stopping and utterly strange last line. That juxtaposition of three unlikely images: a man, the sea and chains. The three images leave a haunting triple exposure in my mind of a man who

is also the sea and that sea is bound in chains. This has to be one of the greatest surreal images conceived.

Here is the meeting of three unlikely objects, like Lautréamont's "chance encounter between a sewing machine and an umbrella on an operating table". The sea is bound by chains; it sings and is pulled by the moon but is imprisoned on earth. This is a new way of looking at our planet and the ocean, and the humans bound up with it. Some of Dylan Thomas' poetry is weirdly surreal but it is surrealism of the highest order – strange, disorientating, and bizarre even, yet grounded in the deep reality of the mystery and pathos of our lives.

Cricieth Castle.

Cricieth:
Mental Health in the Work of Dylan Thomas
by Robert Minhinnick

LITERARY
7
TOUR MAP

CABIN WOOD

"Possessed by the skies" ?

Llanystumdwy

Tŷ Newydd

to Pwllheli

CRICIETH

Dylan explored mental health in his writing...

STATION

...for example... LOVE in the ASYLUM & The Hunchback in the PARK

Afon Dwyfor

Llŷn COASTAL path

CASTL

"I may without fail SUFFER the first vision that set FIRE to the stars."

to Porth-madog →

Cricieth Beach

I looked out of the window. The ghosts were back. Usual time and day, they'd come back. This was Penyfai, two miles north of Bridgend, south Wales, say 1960.

The ghosts were patients at two of the three local 'mental hospitals', Glanrhyd (Angleton), Penyfai and Parc Gwyllt. They walked in line up Heol Eglwys, a nurse in civvies leading the way, maybe a nurse at the rear. But it all seemed very relaxed. Traffic was far lighter in those days. Fly the Tŷ Mawr farm dog used to twitch and dream in the middle of the road when the farmers visited the Tavern. A famous pub it used to be, with "the coolest cellar in Glamorgan". A haunted pub too. A local tailor who roomed there reported hearing "something terrible. And straightaway he dropped down dead ..."

The other ghosts, the 'patients' were medicated. Pilled-up, under the 'chemical cosh', in 'chemical straitjackets'. I learned the terminology when my mother was so prescribed. Gradually I had discovered how things were in the village. Half its people worked in the hospitals, 'the asylums.' The other half was treated there. That was the legend. Penyfai, in those days, was famous for its asylums. Strangers thought they knew me when they learned where I came from.

On our walk, one of the newly-termed 'super moons' appeared around 8pm, glimpsed through the Tŷ Newydd tulip tree and intermittent cloud. We had earlier progressed from Cricieth Castle, past Cadwalader's world famous ice cream, on to Cefn Castell, an extraordinary Mediterranean-type eruption in what is surely a position vulnerable to climate change, then along the beach for final readings in the library.

'Love in the Asylum' is a poem to which I had paid little previous attention. But here is Dylan Thomas writing personally about a real woman, "a girl mad as birds", a girl I might have seen "down Doctors' Lane" or in Penyfai hospital grounds. Maybe

in a visiting-room. This was surely a
real girl whom Thomas knew or had
heard about. And although Swansea's
'mentally ill' weren't shifted as far east
as Penyfai, I knew her too. I still do.

A harsh critic might view the language
in 'Love in the Asylum' as clichéd
and of its era: "Strait in the mazed
bed"; "... the imagined oceans of the
male wards"; "Yet raves at her will";
"the madhouse boards". But not me.
It is a powerful experience to read
this flawed, twisting, deeply poignant
poem. The reader feels language
being manipulated in ways it does not
want to go. But go it must as Thomas
proves what modern poetry should be
doing. 'Love in the Asylum' is never

surrealistic but instead demonstrates
Dylan the sheet metal worker, the
glass blower, using words in molten
malleability. Yet typically, this is a
celebratory work.

'The hunchback in the park' is again
about a particular person. If he had
been born earlier it would not have
been difficult to imagine this man "in
his kennel in the dark" classified as a
pauper lunatic.

The reason Thomas was drawn to
the "hunchback" and "the stranger
who has come / to share my room
in the house not right in the head"
was because he was thrilled by
the 'threats' they posed; by their
dangerous differences; by what they

Above: Penyfai Hospital.

added to life, thus enriching it. For the same reason I have written about the 'shell-shocked' and the *twp*. The *twpsyn* remains a stock Welsh dramatic character – see the work of Frank Vickery, performed *ad infinitum* at venues such as Grand Pavilion, Porthcawl, perpetuating exhausted stereotypes.

So what is Dylan Thomas doing with these poems? Why, writing a history of the 'suicide risks', the 'epileptics' and the 'chronics' who created the economy and culture of Penyfai. Which created me. Thomas is painting them 'into life' with daring images. Because words are how Dylan Thomas demonstrated love and learned to understand the teeming world around him.

'Lunatic asylum', 'asylum', 'mental hospital' were the terms we applied for lack of better words. In Penyfai we all knew 'shell-shocked' men who had 'run away' from or 'deserted' the British Army. And yes, we have always been familiar with people we call *'twp'*, because until recently there hasn't been another English or Welsh word we thought ourselves capable of using to describe their lives.

Later, I became familiar with 'schizophrenia' and 'paranoia', and now 'Alzheimer'. In the 1970s in Penyfai my sister and I read the works of psychologists R. D. Laing and Thomas Szasz, one of these now derided, and one (seemingly) moving

Cwmdonkln Park, Swansea

75539. J.V.

from beyond the pale to lauded acceptance. So I listen to the Alzheimic conversations I overhear when visiting my mother in her care home. For the record, her 'diagnosis' is 'paranoid schizophrenia', not Alzheimer's. I find these conversations extraordinary, Beckettian their hilarious misunderstandings, Dylanesque their syntax.

I know the inadequacies of these words and how they are slowly changing. Yet I still use *twp*. A part of my mind values its brutal dismissal, its monosyllable of derision. One blunt vowel wielded like a taser. Maybe it keeps me looking out of that window at Fly dreaming in her sleep.

And at the ghosts.

Unlike 'Love in the Asylum' and 'The hunchback in the park', the words my sister and I exchange with our mother's consultant have an in-built redundancy. But they are as useful as the machine once used in Parc to transmit electro-convulsive therapy, the keys to the locked wards in Glanrhyd. Thus I completely understand Dylan Thomas' "madhouse" and the "nightmarish room".

Because I have lived in that room.

We all have.

It's the world.

Dylan and Caitlin just married.

London Fitzrovia: Portrait of the Artist as a Young Dog by Griff Rhys Jones

LITERARY
· 8 ·
TOUR MAP

Fitzrovia still retains the scrabbling inner city mix that Dylan Thomas plunged into when he first came to London in 1934, where he lived for a while at 12 Fitzroy Street.

He called it "capital punishment". Fitzroy Street and the extension into Charlotte Street has been home to Constable and Walter Sickert. The Camden Town group met here. Saatchi and Saatchi based themselves here in the 1980s. Channel Four followed. The creative centre of Britain lies in these streets, not perhaps the airy-fairy spiritual creative centre, but certainly the Grub Street, hack coterie, commercial, make a living off my wits writers, artists and chancers' creative centre.

It was in Fitzrovia that Dylan met his future wife Caitlin Macnamara in The Wheatsheaf in Rathbone Place, laying his beer-fuddled head in her lap and stealing her away from Augustus John. They took lodgings in Conway Street and he drank in every pub in the district and roamed the restaurants and clubs. He worked at the BBC and played nightly to his amateur audiences across Fitzrovia.

Dylan told the writer Lawrence Durrell that London "gave him the willies". He wrote that it was "an insane city" and it "filled him with terror". His greatest poetry seems to long for the pantheistic energy of nature. But was he as much a London writer as a Welsh one? Sometimes he yearned for escape from "promiscuity, booze, coloured shirts, too much talk too little work," but he kept coming back for another round. There was always a duality to Dylan and his work.

Dylan spent most of the war working in London. But by the end of the Blitz he was beginning to get weary of the city. It wasn't as if this poet grew tired of London it was that London seemed to wear him out. When the "Rimbaud of Cwmdonkin Drive" had first hurried to join his artist friends in their digs, to sleep on floors and to venture slightly nervously into the pubs of literary and artistic renown, Thomas had become addicted to the everlasting party,

Above: The Fitzroy Tavern, Fitzrovia, London.

the hot excitement of the saloon bar, because, as his friend Trevor Hughes noted, in the Fitzroy Tavern, "...Dylan did not want to drink – no he wanted to talk". The landlords of various pubs claim that they never saw him drunk. In the mid-forties he largely stuck to beer. It made him bloated.

By all accounts, there was no single Dylan Thomas loose in London in the 1930s and 1940s. For every account of the "ugly suckling" as Geoffrey Grigson and his friends dubbed him – the sponger, or the weaving drunk – there are others of his excessive generosity with money and his sober dedication to work. He was quite capable of behaving primly in the company of T. S. Eliot and Edith Sitwell and then 'letting the side down' at some gruesome, organised dinner.

Julian MacLaren-Ross remembers that he once suggested they get a bottle in: "'Whisky? In the office?' He seemed absolutely appalled." In the 1940s the two of them wrote propaganda films for the Ministry of Information, but Dylan arrived on time, wore a suit and was liable to work more conscientiously than Julian thought necessary.

That may have changed. Later commentators noted that he would arrive and line up the beers on the bar like soldiers in rank, in order to knock them back. There have been quite a

Arrived. Canvas, paper, book, no money.
Address: 5 Redcliffe STREET, off Redcliffe GARDENS
South Kensington. S., we think; W.IO.
drop us a line, a burning line, informing us
when and where we shall meet; whether you would
care first of all to visit us here, or exactly wha
YOU LIKE. 8"äff)"ée?,,?.;:====:=:+"&&& %/%/%/%

We are frre mos of the time and whether it
would be easier to meet at we rest

Anywhere, or here, or there, we shall be here or
there. Write soon to the poet Janes and the
painter Thomas who would wish-- the mannered pigs--
to see your hand in the RETURN POG

Top: Dylan Thomas' postcard on arrival in London.

Above: Sign in the Fitzroy Tavern.

Left: The Wheatsheaf Pub where he first met Caitlin Macnamara.

few ready to condemn him. Quite a few ready to 'reclaim' his work from his reputation. Quite a few who want us to stop concentrating on his excesses and read the verses. There are not many who seem to have any sympathy for the road he travelled.

Surely, it was the double demands of his life, the curiosity for company, the furious clowning, the infantilism, the immediate and instant affection (exactly the stuff that can irritate quieter more diligent writers and critics), that fuelled his most vivid verse. Why does *Under Milk Wood* continue to enthral

when T. S. Eliot's *The Family Reunion* sits on the shelf? It reaches down. It sets itself amongst ordinary people. It has the public bar and the post office and the chatterbox stranger written all through it. And perhaps a certain straightforward commercial nouse? It was the post-propaganda film Dylan who wrote that work.

Dylan disdained the label of surrealist, but his characters use their fantasies to free themselves from the buttoned-up village and its closed minds. In the streets of Llareggub they gossip, sniff and sneer, but in their private

Right: *Memoirs of the Forties* by Julian MacLaren-Ross; *18 Poems* inscribed by Dylan Thomas to John Arlott.

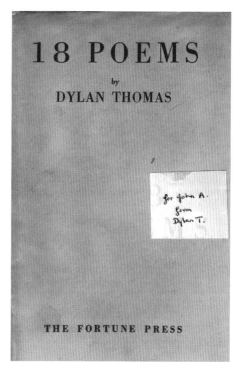

soliloquies they lust and seethe with forbidden desire. There were no small town constraints in Fitzrovia. An artist could properly lead the Bohemian life, alongside nude models, raucous painters and their mistresses, and the "regulars, wits and bums" that the writer Julian MacLaren-Ross described.

Dylan Thomas was not a household name until 1945 and the success of his collection of poems *Deaths and Entrances*. Before that, he was known to (and part of) an informed circle. He worked in a recognizable world of the freelance media creative dogsbody. Journalism was not his métier. Instead he picked up propaganda films or bits of short story. Perhaps today he would have written television, then he worked for the radio, and as much as an actor or 'voice' as a writer, turning

out for the radio producer Douglas Cleverdon, but also for John Arlott, later the cricket commentator, who cast him often and seldom had cause to complain of lateness or indifference. By the late 1940s Dylan was making 20 radio appearances a year, turning up to read or as a critic or a guest on a panel.

Fitzrovia was important to Dylan Thomas, even if it wasn't always conducive to his productivity. Still, he managed to bash out frequent flashes of genius while in the city, and is remembered in its bookshops and theatres as much as he is by the sundry boozers proclaiming his name on plaques. Fitzrovia was also where he met his future wife and a stepping stone to the even brighter lights of New York.

Aerial photo of Swansea 1940s.

Swansea:

The Pacifist, the Propagandist and the Swansea Blitz
by Peter Stead

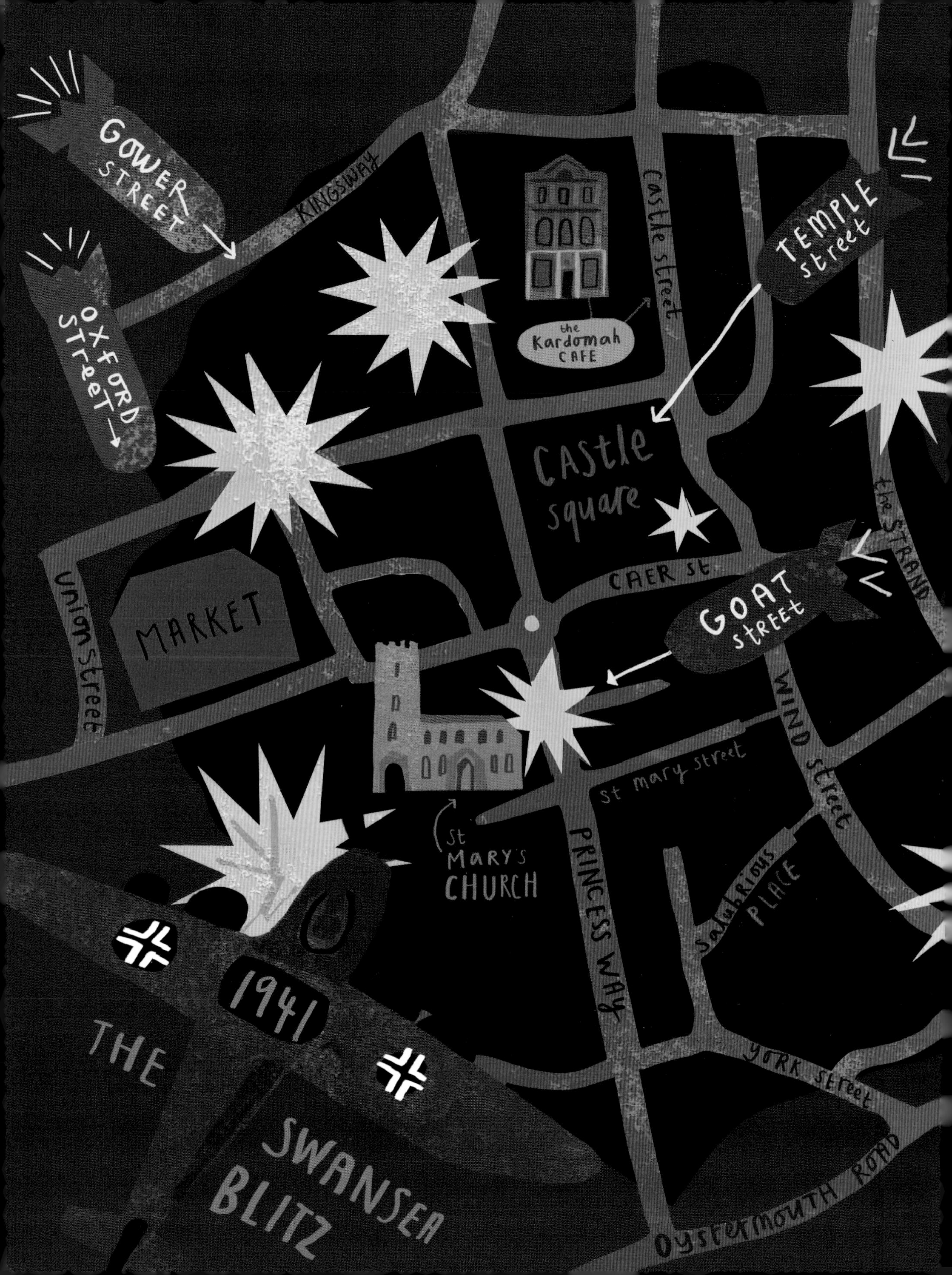

THE
SWANSEA
BLITZ

1941

GOWER
STREET

OXFORD
STREET

KINGSWAY

Castle street

the Kardomah CAFE

TEMPLE
Street

CASTLE
square

CAER st

the STRAND

MARKET

Union Street

GOAT
Street

St MARY'S
CHURCH

St mary street

WIND street

PRINCESS WAY

SALUBRIOUS PLACE

YORK street

OYSTERMOUTH ROAD

"OUR SWANSEA has DIED"

! MUSEUM

On a cold February morning in 1941, as the firemen cleared up the centre of Swansea after a third consecutive night of devastating German bombing, Bert Trick bumped into his friends Dylan and Caitlin.

He reported that, as the three of them contemplated the blackened entrails of what had once been Swansea Market, Dylan said with tears in his eyes, "our Swansea has died".

For students and biographers of Dylan this story has become a useful way of reminding readers that Dylan had moved on. Since 1934 he had been more visitor than resident of Swansea, and since their marriage in 1937, the largely itinerant Dylan and Caitlin stayed with his parents at nearby Bishopston, rather than Swansea, when they came to town. The story also serves to explain the degree to which an evocation of Swansea now became an increasingly important and memorable feature of Dylan's writing and, more particularly, his broadcasting. Swansea had been a vital component of *Portrait of the Artist as a Young Dog*, his 1940 evocation of childhood, but that book had not set out to specifically

define Dylan as a Swansea writer. That process came after 1941 in his broadcasts and crucially in his radio play 'Return Journey'.

Dylan Thomas

Return Journey to Swansea
performed by Dylan Thomas and supporting cast

and
Dylan Thomas reading the poetry of
Betjeman · Bogan · Boland · Gogarty
Graves · MacDonagh · Manifold · Plomer
Reed · Edward Thomas

In post war decades the citizens of Swansea contemplated the changing nature of their town. There was a growing sense that, for all the social improvements, the Blitz of 1941 had destroyed crucial aspects of

Above: Untitled painting of the bank, Temple Street, Swansea, following the Blitz, by Will Evans (1888-1957), 1941 (watercolour, pencil and crayon on paper).

Right: *Swansea's Blitz* by Will Evans.

Swansea's identity. People who had known the old Swansea frequently argued that Swansea had lost much of its distinctiveness and most of its distinction. Earlier visitors to the town had appreciated its intimately crowded centre in which medieval, eighteenth century and Victorian structures stood side by side, and in which a historic and flourishing market, modern stores of real elegance and a host of theatres and cinemas catered for all tastes and pockets.

The notion that in the Blitz something had 'died' became commonplace, but it also endowed Dylan with a special place as a champion of Swansea. It was generally appreciated that in his notebooks the young Dylan had accumulated the poetic capital that would serve him throughout his short life. In time, the study of Dylan's prose revealed the extent to which his rounded personality, his language, his humour, his urbanity and his sheer humanity was shaped by the manner in which he fed off the personality and distinction of his town. When he first left home, he referred to the "queer Swansea world... a world, that thank Christ, was self-sufficient". Caitlin was of the view that wherever he went, he took his favourite elements of Swansea with him. To contemplate Dylan in the context of the old Swansea is to confront the essence and soul of both.

Today the old Swansea town centre is barely recognisable. Wind Street, perhaps the last reminder of the Edwardian town, used to be a street of hotels and businesses that catered for visitors to Swansea's cosmopolitan waterfront. It is now full of bars and restaurants. One can still appreciate the medieval origins of the town in Castle Square (for centuries past the heart of Swansea and still holds remains of the Norman castle) and how royal, feudal, ecclesiastical and civic authority emanated from this spot. And it was precisely here that Dylan developed his sense of what made Swansea tick. As a young reporter he was based in the newspaper office built adjacent to the Castle and just across the road were The Three Lamps pub and the Kardomah Café, where Dylan and his friends debated global, cultural and political issues. This is the place to read 'Return Journey', Dylan's epitaph for his own youth and a commemoration of the sheer intensity of daily life generated in this small pocket of urban Wales.

And this too is the place to consider the Blitz that had destroyed so much of Dylan's self-sufficient world. The destruction of Ben Evans, Swansea's most elegant departmental store; the Kardomah Café and the surrounding streets had been the most spectacular

Sign on the 'No Sign
Wine Bar' on Wind
Street; Salubrious
passage off Wind
Street; Gower
Heritage Centre
tour bus; The Three
Lamps.

and photogenic aspect of the three-
night Blitz. To this day the photographs
taken immediately after the Blitz have
lost none of their shocking power.
Historic streets such as Goat Street
and College Street had gone, as had
major stores, a synagogue, a chapel,
over 50 hotels, pubs and restaurants.
The market, the Grammar School
and St. Mary's Church had been
substantially damaged. In all 387
people were killed in the bombing of
Swansea.

Dylan himself was shaped by the
War. His friends the composer Daniel
Jones and poet Vernon Watkins assure
us that there was nothing political

about Dylan, but in the 1930s all
his contact with Bert Trick and the
intellectual left in Swansea would
have confirmed his anti-militarism.
Given his fascination with death, it
was not surprising that he became
an acclaimed war poet. He had
witnessed the beginning of the London
Blitz and after Swansea he was soon
encountering the destruction of other
cities. His war poems brilliantly and
succinctly transformed the local and
specific into the universal. Meanwhile
he found wartime employment as a
documentary scriptwriter and this
was fitting indeed for the lifelong
filmgoer. The British Documentary
Film Movement played a crucial part in

cementing the validity of 'the People's War' and Dylan's involvement in this significant moment for British popular culture clinched his own role both as a communicator and as a writer with a social hinterland.

Caitlin dancing.

Caitlin Thomas' Aeron Valley:

Mother Love in the Aeron Valley
by George Tremlett

CAITLIN stayed here while Dylan was away in LONDON

home of

William & Vera Killick

Plas y GELLI

Llundain Fach

Afon Aeron

to Aberaeron

B4342

Talsarn

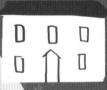
The Vale of Aeron

The Red Lion

Felinfach

Caitlin borrowed Ponies from Pentrefelin FARM She also DANCED every day

B4342

LAMPETER ROAD

B4331

Farmed by
DAN THOMAS
poet and teacher

entrefelin FARM

Abermeurig

ylan ame to visit from he City

Legend has it that Dylan Thomas' only daughter, Aeronwy, was conceived on the banks of the River Aeron in Ceredigion, but she did not believe it and neither did her mother.

"I don't think so," said Aeronwy, when I asked her.

"Not very likely," replied Caitlin, when I was staying at her home in Catania, Sicily, in 1985, working together on her memoirs.

However, the Thomases did stay briefly in the Aeron Valley in 1942, but at that time, they had a home – an apartment at 8 Wentworth Studios, Manresa Road, just off Kings Road, then and now one of the more exclusive parts of Chelsea, particularly popular with London's artists. On one side, their neighbour was the writer and artist Mervyn Peake; on the other, the painter John Grome, who later established a studio in Rome.

Since autumn 1941, Dylan had been employed as a scriptwriter for Strand Films, earning £8 a week to work up documentaries for the Ministry of Information. He travelled with film crews to different parts of Britain including Bradford, Coventry, Glasgow and Birmingham, adapting scripts as needed.

While he was away, Caitlin would go to Wales, staying either at Laugharne Castle with Frances Hughes (whose husband Richard Hughes, had joined the Admiralty) or at Plas y Gelli at Talsarn with Vera Killick (née Phillips), whose husband was out in Greece fighting with the partisans.

When he returned after filming out of town, Dylan often stayed in London rather than join Caitlin in Wales (some of his embarrassed apologies for not going west to see her can be found in *Dylan Thomas: The Collected Letters* edited by Paul Ferris) – but it shouldn't be assumed that there were any great tensions in the marriage.

The simplest explanations are often the right ones, even with the Thomases. For the first time since leaving the *Swansea Evening Post*,

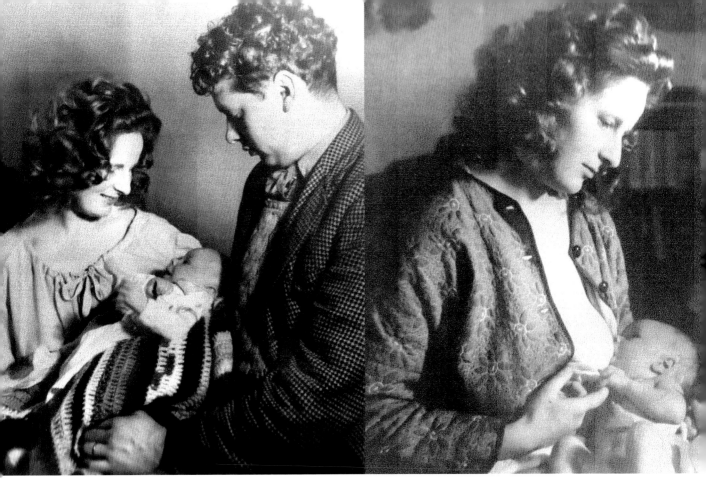

Above left to right:
Caitlin, Dylan and
new baby Aeronwy.

Right: Caitlin
dancing.

Dylan was working office hours and
couldn't always get back to Wales at
weekends if he had to be back at his
desk on Monday morning.

However, in the summer of 1942, his
employer at Strand Films, Donald
Taylor, told him he could take time
away from the office to write the film
script *Wales – Green Mountain, Black
Mountain*. It's quite probable
that Aeronwy was conceived then,
at Plas y Gelli.

Throughout their marriage, Caitlin
never disturbed Dylan when he was
writing; he had his life and she had
hers. While at Plas y Gelli she would
dance every day and, later, borrow one
of the ponies at Pentrefelin Farm and

ride off down the valley.

Dancing was always important to her;
she trained in Paris, worked briefly
in London revues and continued to
practise into her old age. On the four
occasions I stayed with Caitlin in Sicily,
she spent two hours every morning,
from 8am to 10am, bathing and
exercising.

One day I asked her a question about
ballet and she immediately ran
through her daily routine, rhythmically
bending, twisting and touching her
toes at the age of 74.

Her love for horses came from a
childhood spent in the New Forest with
her sisters Nicolette and Brigid, their

brother John and Augustus John's children. They followed the Hunt, riding wild like ragamuffins; dressed up for pony shows and gymkhanas. It was often Caitlin who won the trophies, for she would tackle any fence even when she was terrified.

"I was wild," she told me, and when you have had a childhood like that it never leaves you.

The following year Caitlin spent much more time in the safety of Talsarn. Aeronwy was born in London on 3 March 1943 and their home in Wentworth Studios had a glass roof. With the German raids on London expected to intensify, both agreed it would be safer for Caitlin to take

Aeronwy to Plas y Gelli again.

Dylan joined her there sometimes, but not very often, and Caitlin did not mind. She hadn't seen her son Llewelyn since autumn 1941 and was plagued by guilt as she felt she had abandoned him. She had left him with her mother Yvonne Macnamara and sister Brigid in a desperate attempt to save her marriage, (as described in our book *Caitlin: A Warring Absence*). Now she threw herself back into motherhood.

"I was totally bound up with Aeronwy," Caitlin told me. "I had wanted a girl, and when she arrived I wanted to be with her all the time; feed her, hold her close in my arms, wash her and

comb her hair ... I was always combing her hair ... God had given me what I wanted, and I wasn't really bothered whether Dylan came down or not, for motherhood the second time around brought something out in me that I hadn't felt when Llewelyn was born."

If Caitlin's reference to God sounds a little unexpected, I would only say this; when I was staying with her in Catania, she initially pooh-poohed any question of her and Dylan's religious beliefs, but one night she took me to see Catania Cathedral, which is dedicated to Saint Agatha, who was born and martyred there.

Above: Caitlin, Dylan and daughter Aeronwy.

Left, top: The start of the Dylan Thomas Trail from Aberaeron to New Quay, Ceredigion, west Wales.

Left, bottom: Aeron Valley, Ceredigion.

As I wandered around the cathedral, which partly dates to the eleventh century, and yet is also gloriously baroque, we became temporarily separated and I found her on her knees, before a statue of the Virgin Mary, crossing herself as Catholics do. The following day, when we were talking on our own, I told her what I had seen and asked her again about both her and Dylan's religious beliefs.

"I have always loved the Mother and Child tradition, which is very deep in the Mediterranean culture," said Caitlin, adding "I love the baby Jesus" before telling me how deeply she bonded with Aeronwy and then later with Colm.

"I let Llewelyn down very badly," she said. "That will always be on my conscience ... and I felt I'd been given a second chance."

Does all this explain why, here in the Aeron Valley 70 years ago, she and Dylan, forever walking, talking, and sharing the landscape around them, found peace in wartime, and the metaphors and sense of purpose that make *Wales – Green Mountain, Black Mountain* so powerful?

New Quay Ceredigion,
west Wales.

Ceredigion Coast:
Llareggub and the Black Lion
by Samantha Wynne-Rhydderch

Dylan wrote in the Apple House

Plas Llanina

The year that Dylan Thomas lived in New Quay (September 1944 – July 1945) he rented a bungalow called Majoda[1] looking over towards the terraces of stern houses sheltered from the wind in the arm of Pengraig Hill (the "hill of windows" in *Under Milk Wood*).

If Dylan wanted any kind of social life he would have had to walk the mile and a half into the town, either along the New Road, or else across the beach if the tide was right, or follow one of the little paths just above the cliff edge. If he was pushing Aeronwy in a pram, then the road would have been the easier option. This route took him past my grandparents' house, Hafod Arthen and most days, my newly-retired grandfather barely into his 40s after 30 years at sea, was to be found in a shed at the foot of his steep garden overlooking the road and the bay beyond. He would wave and say hello to Dylan and Dylan would call back "Good morning, Captain", a common refrain as Dylan walked around New Quay, the town that was home to over 35 retired and serving sea captains during the war. [2]

When you walk around a place on a regular basis you encounter it in quite an intimate way. You see people in their front windows or gardens or parks. In a small place you see the same people doing the same thing all the time. And they see you. Which meant that if you ambled past my grandparents' house pushing a pram with a squeaky wheel, then Grandpa, who could turn his hand to anything on board ship, was going to come out and fix it. With barely ten years difference in age between these two men, one of whom had just retired and the other about to embark on a new stage in his career, the practical man struck up a conversation with the impractical one, the man who had crossed the Atlantic several times over with the one who was about to make that journey several times and not return after only his fourth visit.

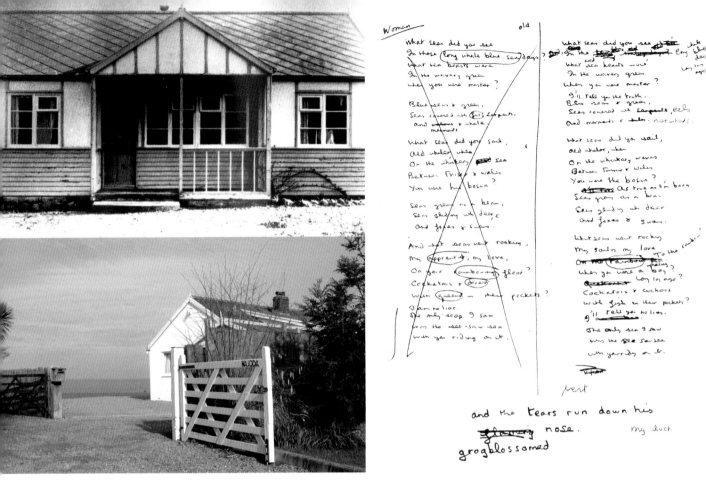

Above: Majoda then and Majoda now; *Under Milk Wood* draft.

Why does this chance conversation over a broken pram wheel matter? It seems to me that Dylan needed company that was both cosmopolitan and local at the same time. New Quay in those days was a place where both those elements blended seamlessly. In contrast to most of the rest of Wales, half of New Quay's inhabitants had sailed around the globe several times over, and behind their front doors hung textiles and languages and spices rarely seen in other parts of the UK. It is an unlikely form of feeling at home. Every day for a year Dylan would walk past houses with names like Brisbane Villa, Falkland and Zenobia, and every day for a year chat to sea captains who were more familiar with the back streets of Shanghai and Rio than they were with nearby villages like Llanarth and Llandysul. Not only are the houses of New Quay named after cities on the other side of the world, thrown into this mix are houses named after rivers in Brazil (Paranà) or counties you can see miles away across the water (Gwynedd) or concepts (Tangnefedd = peace) or ships (Confidence). There are even whole areas of New Quay that are informally called after difficult sea passages in other parts of the world. For example, walking round the front of New Quay (by the Blue Bell pub) is known as *rowndio'r Horn* (going round the Horn) because you can be hit by the fiercest of winds. And this is barely feet away from a little stone

wall known as Cnwc y Glep (literally 'chatting corner') where the retired sea captains would come to share their tales and keep an eye on what was going on in the bay (and several of them were used to meeting in ports in far corners of the world, let alone in New Quay). Nowadays it is fishermen and yacht owners who sit there to swap yarns.

After walking along the New Road on his way into New Quay, Dylan would pass the Emporium, a sweet shop like Miss Price's in *Under Milk Wood*, and Brooklands (now called Eastcliffe), the home of Walter Cherry and his son-in-law, builder Dan Cherry Jones (Cherry Owen was a carpenter in *Under Milk Wood*). And he'd pass Manchester House, a draper's like Mog Edwards' in *Under Milk Wood*. Opposite the draper's is Arnant, where Glanmor Rees, brother of the New Quay historian, Myra Evans had his cobbler's shop on the lower ground floor. Several residents in New Quay have mentioned to me over the years

that Glanmor was a sociable, educated chap and that Dylan would pop in for a chat on the affairs of the world and of New Quay before making his way to one of the town's watering holes. Dylan would almost certainly have sometimes walked into New Quay along Brongwyn Lane, which runs parallel to the New Road, where there used to be a farm called Maesgwyn (roughly translates as 'white field') long since washed into the sea. Indeed in *Under Milk Wood*, one of the fourth drowned asks "Who milks the cows in Maesgwyn?". When Dylan reached the Black Lion, he would have an audience and friend in landlord Jack Patrick Evans, so well read he had a special arrangement with the library enabling him to borrow ten books a week [3]. Around this pub shone a constellation of characters with a love of literature and witty conversation including Aberaeron vet Thomas Herbert, Alistair Graham (thought to be the model for Sebastian Flyte in *Brideshead Revisited*), and locals

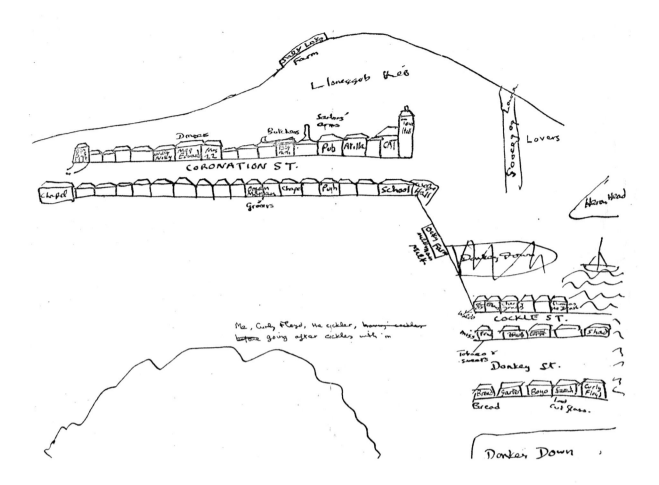

Left: New Quay, Ceredigion.

Above: Dylan's map of Llareggub – based on New Quay.

Captain John Davies and Captain Tom Polly as well as Griff Jenkins senior, my maternal grandmother's first husband.

This cocktail of places and spices and captains just in off the boat from Australia or about to board a tanker to Chile gave a special energy to life in New Quay. I think the mix of sea captains and literary landlords suited Dylan's desire for conviviality but also provided somewhere quiet enough to produce work as lasting and original as *Under Milk Wood*.

[1] In 1999 I met John Evans, whose father had rented the bungalow to Dylan and he told me that the name of the bungalow was a composite of the names of himself and his sister (Majorie) and his brother (David)

[2] *The Dylan Thomas Trail* by David N. Thomas (Y Lolfa, 2002), p. 68

[3] *Dylan Thomas: A Farm, Two Mansions and A Bungalow* by David N. Thomas (Seren, 2000), p. 83

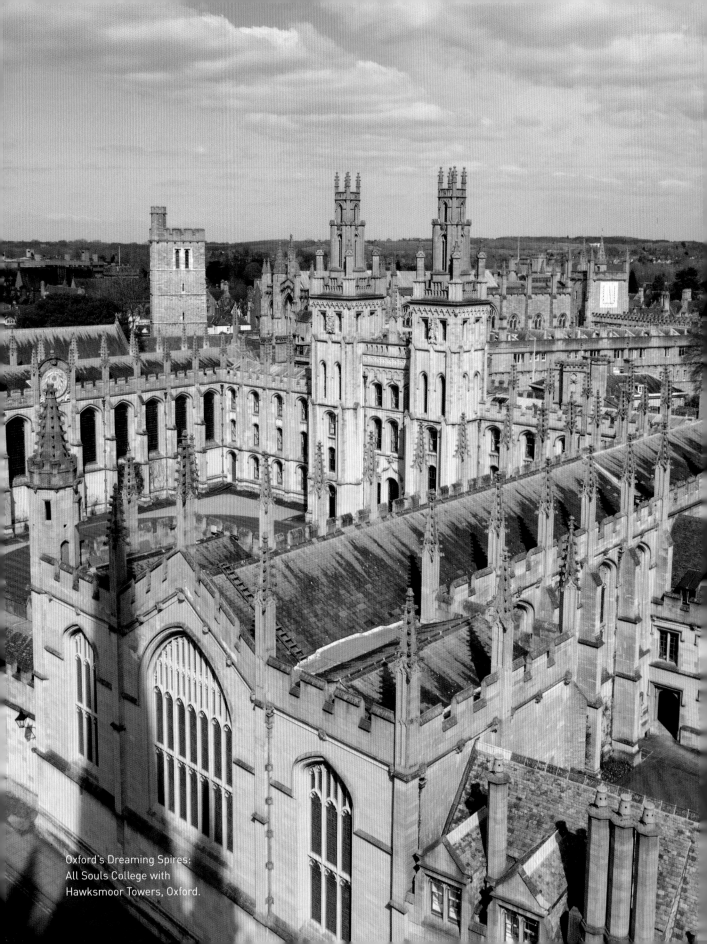

Oxford's Dreaming Spires:
All Souls College with
Hawksmoor Towers, Oxford.

Oxford and South Leigh:

Dreaming Spires and Country Living
by Andrew Lycett

VISITED by Dylan, investigating
The Mistletoe Bough Legend

Minster LOVELL

Witney

this way out of town towards Dylan's rural Oxfordshire haunts...

South Leigh

The Trout Inn

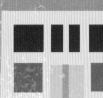

St Giles'

Parks Road

Dylan moved here in 1947... his local pub was The Mason's Arms

he also cycled to The Fleece in Witney

St Cross Road

Magdalen COLLEGE

Hollywell Street

Longwall Street

Queen's LANE

[] The Gloucester Arms

The Turf TAVERN

HIGH STREET

Oxford

Dylan lived here 1946-1947

to

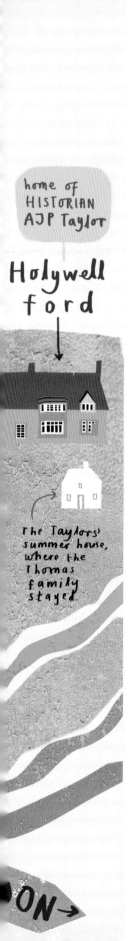

home of HISTORIAN AJP Taylor

Holywell ford

The Taylors' summer house, where the Thomas family stayed

They are the least celebrated years of Dylan Thomas' brief life – the ones he spent in the city and environs of Oxford between 1946 and 1949, as he negotiated the difficult transition between the frenzy of existence in London during the Second World War and his return to the tranquillity of his Welsh homeland to live in Laugharne.

But this was not a wasted period. Dylan was in great demand as a multi-faceted contributor to the BBC. He worked hard, regularly taking the train to London, where he also wrote scripts for Gainsborough and Ealing film studios. Particularly after he went to live in South Leigh, nine miles west of Oxford, he enjoyed, perhaps for the first time, a proper family life, mixing with villagers and absorbing material which, it is now clear, helped in the genesis of his great play for voices *Under Milk Wood*.

In an ideal world Dylan Thomas might have gone to Oxford himself, as an undergraduate. His schoolmaster father had taken a first class degree at Aberystwyth and would have loved his son to study there, or even at Oxford.

But, for all his intellectual precocity, Dylan was not academic material. He was first sighted in Oxford in November 1941 when the young poet Sidney Keyes (soon to lose his life in the war) invited him to address the English Club. Philip Larkin, a student at St John's, remembered him appreciatively:

"Hell of a fine man: little, snubby, hopelessly pissed bloke who made hundreds of cracks and read parodies of everybody in appropriate voices."

In March 1946, shortly after the publication of *Deaths and Entrances*, his fourth and most eclectic collection of poems, Dylan returned to live in

with no running water, although there was gas and electricity. His two children Llewelyn and Aeronwy had to sleep in the main house with the Taylors.

But Dylan was in easy commuting distance of London's Paddington Station and the BBC. When in Oxford he made a name for himself, both in donnish circles and among the wider student population, propping up the bars in pubs such as the Turf Tavern, the George Hotel and the Gloucester Arms (he also enjoyed a club called White's near the bus station, and was known to make his way out to the Perch and Trout inns by the river).

He wrote an affectionate (though unpublished) poem about the university in which he muses on what might have been. It begins: "Oxford I sing, though in untutored tones, alack!/I heard, long years ago, her call, but blew it back". And it carries on: "Ah, not for me the windblown scarf,/ The bicycle to the Trout, the arm-in-arm sweatered swing, Marx in a punt, Firbank aloud round the gas-ring".

the university town – at the unlikely invitation of Margaret Taylor, wife of the historian Alan (A. J. P.) Taylor, whom he had met a decade earlier.

She offered Dylan and his young family the summerhouse attached to Holywell Ford, the Taylors' own dwelling in the grounds of Magdalen College. This "converted ark", as Dylan described it, wasn't palatial. But he had nowhere else to go. Situated beside a small stream, it was damp

He couldn't stay forever at Holywell Ford. He had hoped at one stage to find another cottage in the grounds of Magdalen, but that didn't materialise. So, after spending some months in Italy in the summer of 1947, courtesy of a Society of Authors grant arranged by his friend Edith Sitwell, Margaret Taylor fixed him up with a new place to live – the grand-sounding Manor House in the village of South Leigh near Eynsham.

Once again the facilities were sparse, with no electricity or inside lavatory.

Most of the mains water was drawn off by a cattle drinking trough halfway up the drive. But there were compensations. In those days the village had a railway, which meant Dylan could easily travel to Oxford and London (Bill Mitchell, the station master, would keep the train waiting if he saw Dylan heaving into view). A lively social life centred on the village pub, the Mason's Arms, where Dylan was known for his skills at the pub game shove ha'penny. The village itself was notorious for its independent-minded and often cantankerous residents often cited as the inspiration for the characters from *Under Milk Wood*.

Left: Grounds of Magdalen College, Oxford, where Dylan and his family lived in 1946.

Above: South Leigh Station.

Caitlin became close friends with Cordelia Sewell, who had been at the Slade School of Art and knew her sister Nicolette. The two neighbours were soon in and out of each other's houses, often venturing further afield, since Cordelia's friends, the Colgroves from nearby Stanton Harcourt, owned a van which facilitated visits to surrounding villages.

Dylan often travelled by bicycle to The Fleece, a pub in nearby Witney. This provided the unlikely location for a roving BBC programme he introduced called 'Country Magazine', about the Windrush Valley.

Although Dylan was busy working on radio and film scripts, and made advances in writing *Under Milk Wood*, his main poetic achievement in this period was the long and complex 'In Country Sleep', the first draft of which was written in Italy. In an effort to improve his productivity, Margaret Taylor gave him a gypsy caravan so he could work in a field next to Manor House, untroubled by family demands.

Occasionally Dylan's Oxford student friends made their way to South Leigh. He spent a boozy day with Paul Redgrave, from St Catherine's College, investigating the Mistletoe Bough legend in Minster Lovell, five miles from South Leigh.

After an unsuccessful attempt to locate this reputed local provenance of an ancient folk tale, they ended back at Redgrave's cottage at Church Hanborough, where Dylan was so fascinated by the story of a poltergeist in the local church that he insisted on reading one of John Donne's sermons from the pulpit there.

In March 1949 he embarked on another foreign trip – to Czechoslovakia, and when he returned, his agreeable experiment with English university and country life was over. He moved to Laugharne, where the ever-attentive Margaret Taylor had bought him the Boathouse; the ideal poet's residence, overlooking the Taf Estuary in Carmarthenshire, which has since become the most potent visible symbol of his life and career.

Laugharne,
Carmarthenshire.

Dylan Thomas' Laugharne:
The Boathouse, The Pelican and Brown's Hotel
by Chris Moss

LITERARY · 13 · TOUR MAP

LAUGHARNE:
"This timeless, beautiful, BARMY town"

Saint Martin's CHURCH

Dylan's grave

Dylan's *local*

Brown's HOTEL

Dylan's parents lived at The PELICAN

Clifton street

newbridge Road

Victoria street

Duncan Street

Sea view

'The Map of LOVE' collection was written here

Dylan's Walk

WOGAN street

River CORAN

Laugharne CASTLE

Painter Augustus John CHASED Dylan around the castle grounds ... for SEDUCING CAITLIN

water st

Eros

Rent: 10 shillings per week

Gosport street

the STRAND

Sir John's Hill

this way

The Taf Estuary

'My sea-shaken house on a break neck of rocks'

BOAT HOUSE

writing SHED

the Heron's EYE view

"Off and on, up and down, high and dry, man and boy, I've been living now for 15 years, or centuries, in this timeless, beautiful, barmy (both spellings) town..."*

He is buried at St Martin's Church, in the new graveyard to the right of the steep cobbled road, beneath a uPVC cross that he shares with his one great love. Because literary pilgrims are morbid souls, it is here that they come to pay their respects, read some verse, do whatever they do.

There are, though, many far better places to catch the poet at work and at play.

Dylan Thomas first came to Laugharne in 1934 with his friend, schoolmaster Glyn Jones. They came tramping over the bosky, beautiful Llansteffan peninsula, where his aunt had a farm, Fernhill, to take the small boat across the Taf estuary to the old Ferry House.

He penned a letter to Pamela Hansford Johnson:

"I wish I could describe what I am looking on ... a hopeless, fallen angel of a day it is ... I can never do justice ... to the miles and miles and miles of mud and gray sand, to the un-nerving silence of the fisherwomen, & the mean-souled cries of the gulls & the herons."

Pamela was his first love, and his lyricism was as much for her as for his discovery. But Laugharne has a history of beguiling writers. Samuel Coleridge, Mary Wollstonecraft and Edward Thomas all spent time here; but each writer must believe he is a pioneer, and that reality challenges his art, and if the tucked-away town tested the young Thomas' descriptive powers then that was all to the good.

In 1936, he attended the Eisteddfod in Fishguard, where he got blind drunk with artist Augustus John. Afterwards they travelled to Laugharne to visit Richard Hughes (the celebrated author

*From 'Laugharne', a prose poem recorded on 5 October 1953 for Aneirin Talfan Davies for the BBC's Welsh Home Service and broadcast on 5 November 1953 – the day Thomas became gravely ill in New York.

Above, left to right: Augustus John and Caitlin; The Boathouse.

Right: Dylan's 'Spontaneous Laugharne Poem' on the back of a Laugharne postcard; Dylan Thomas' writing shed, Laugharne.

of *High Wind in Jamaica*), who resided in the grand Castle House and kept a good wine cellar. Thomas was trying to seduce the painter's young 'girlfriend', Caitlin, inviting her to join him in the back seat of John's big black car for a canoodle. Unwilling to play cuckold, John chased Thomas around the battlements of the castle. It was a moment of joyous madness, youth pursued by age, poet versus painter.

After binging on kisses and vintage Burgundy, Thomas returned to Swansea, travelled on to London, and then went west again, this time to Cornwall to make official his affair with Caitlin, whom he married in Penzance on 11 July 1937.

In the spring of the following year,

Richard Hughes helped the Thomases to find a house in Laugharne: Eros, a fisherman's cottage for which he and Caitlin paid ten shillings a week. Perched over the boggiest part of the estuary, a morass which floods during spring tides, they could see the cockler women walking out to work and men paddling smacks to catch flatfish.

Eros was a damp, dark two-up, two-down. Dylan wrote to poet Henry Treece that the double bed sounded like a "swing band with coffin, oompah, slush-pump, gob-stick and almost wakes the deaf, syphilitic neighbours". There was no running water and they had to go to the loo on the foreshore.

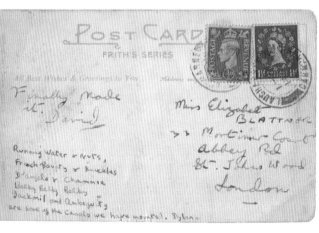

LHN 2]   LAUGHARNE, KING STREET   Copyright
Frith's

If he was envious of the Hughes' opulent lifestyle, he didn't show it, the poor poet used the castle precinct as his back garden and found a certain peace in Laugharne. He read widely, kept on top of the reviews, and corresponded with editors. In July the Thomases were able to move to the more stately Sea View, where Thomas wrote *The Map of Love*. Augustus John popped in and reported to a friend that "the Thomases live in frightful squalor and hideousness". But Dylan had friendship and support in the Williams family, a Laugharne dynasty that owned the local electricity generator, the bus company and some 50 houses (acquired at bargain-rates through the medieval Corporation), as well as Brown's Hotel – one of several boisterous, boozy pubs Dylan Thomas retired to between drafts and the domestic duties he couldn't avoid. His and Caitlin's first child, Llewelyn, was born in 1939.

The war and gainful work interrupted this sojourn and the Thomases were compelled to lead something of a gypsy life, going up and down to London, dropping in to see his parents and old friends at Swansea and Caitlin's mother in Hampshire, and relocating for short spells to Oxford and Ceredigion, but Laugharne must have stayed on his mind as something different from all of these, something

Below: Laugharne
Castle gazebo.

that stayed put and harboured its
energies in the slow tides.

In April 1949, Dylan's generous patron
Margaret Taylor bought the Boathouse
for £2,500 and gifted it as a home for
Dylan, Caitlin and their two children
(Aeronwy had been born in London in
1943). With its splendid views over the
estuary and Sir John's Hill, and an old
garage that Dylan was able to use as a
writing shed, this was as close as the
Thomases would get to a dream home.

Now he could settle down and let
Laugharne's loud, rough folk and the
quiet, calm drama of its landscape
work for him. Seas and rivers flow in
his later poems, as do the waters of
the body. He wrote 'Do not go gentle

into that good night', one of the finest
villanelles in the English language. He
conceived and began to craft *Under
Milk Wood*, which is, among many
other things, an exuberant evocation
of daily life in "the strangest town in
Wales".

He also enjoyed the views from the
Laugharne Castle gazebo, where he
could see over to the Llansteffan and
Gower peninsulas, and wrote much of
his short story collection inspired by
his childhood, *Portrait of the Artist as
a Young Dog*.

Colm, the Thomases' third and final
child, was born in July 1949. Aeronwy's
memoir, *My Father's Places* speaks
of picnics on the foreshore and Caitlin

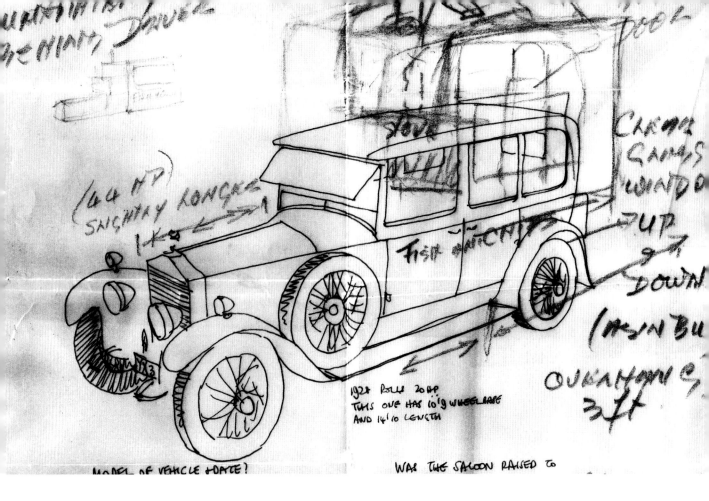

Above: The Rolls Royce Chippie Van, Laugharne.

Right: Dylan's grave, St Martin's Church, Laugharne.

bathing, nude, close to the old chapel at Faulkner's Lawn. When he moved his parents into The Pelican, a house (and former inn) opposite Brown's Hotel, Dylan finally had his loved ones around him. After all the bright lights and busyness of London (and, during his last few years, he travelled to New York and to Iran) there was something attractive about a village-sized town "with good pubs, little law and no respect".

That the poet is buried in Laugharne might be sentimentally saleable, but good pilgrims – and that means those who have captured that strange mingling of life and death that takes place in so many of his poems – will wander aimlessly around the township in search of the Dylan Thomas who didn't go gently in any direction or at any time of the day.

Dylan Thomas and his family, Laugharne.

The Thomas Children's Laugharne

The Rats and Mably the Dog

by Hannah Ellis

LITERARY
· 14 ·
TOUR MAP

Faulkner's LAWN

BOAThouse

writing SHED

The Pelican

BROWNS Hotel

Clifton Street

THE THOMAS FAMILY

Newbridge Road

VICTORIA street

Duncan St.   Market Lane

Sea View

Dylan's WALK

WOGAN street

Water st

the ESTUARINE GRASSES

Dylan

stories

GAMES

Llewelyn   Aeron

Dolly

frogmore St

Gosport st

the STRAND

LAUGHARNE

picnics

"It looked heavenly: a place to explore, to run around, where we would be living forever. It had verandas and balconies, water-butts, stepped gardens, a large boat shed in the back yard, the harbour and a wall protecting us from the wilds of the friendly estuary beyond. We had fallen upon paradise." *My Father's Places*, Aeronwy Thomas

In September 2009, 60 years to the day that my mum had first seen the Boathouse, we scattered her ashes there, allowing her to join the herons, gulls and pipers that still encircle the house on stilts.

It was at that point that my own discovery about my family began. I had given birth three weeks earlier and was a bundle of conflicting emotions, caused by hormones, lack of sleep and grief. We had arrived at the Boathouse and walked with difficulty down what appeared to be the never-ending steep steps. My husband was protectively carrying our tiny son, and I was still suffering from the sciatica that had plagued me during pregnancy. Predictably, my son immediately filled a nappy and then screamed for food.

As I was sitting on the chaise longue in the sitting room feeding my son, I wondered what it must have been like for my family living here, years earlier in post-war Laugharne, without the benefits and luxuries of modern life.

A few days later, I decided to read my mother, Aeron Thomas' warm and sincere memoir, *My Father's Places* about living in Laugharne between the ages of six and ten. In my grandfather's letters he shows genuine affection towards his daughter but often includes comments that would suggest that she was a spirited individual such as "sweet fiend Aeron" or "... live noisily with Aeron." Certainly her memoirs demonstrate that, though delicate and tiny for her age, she was a feisty

Above: A young Aeron.

Right: The Boathouse.

and independent child. She admits to 'poisoning' a Swedish student in an act of revenge, encouraging her friends to ring their bicycle bells, sing and bark with the family dog Mably as they passed outside her father's writing shed, and stubbornly refusing to be called Dylan Thomas' daughter; "'I'm Aeron Thomas,' I corrected calmly. 'Dylan Thomas' daughter is not a name', I thought, in a fury of indignation." Her book has been an invaluable resource for me to visualise a typical (or should that be atypical) day at the Boathouse, and has given me the chance to meet the quirky and colourful characters that turned it into a home.

In my mind's eye, I enter the Boathouse from the original steps, which are just along from the ones they use now, and I see a bucket full of cockles soaking in salt water, waiting to be fried up for lunch. This was one of my grandfather's favourite dishes. The cockles would either be cooked by my grandmother Caitlin with enough garlic and pepper to make you sneeze, or doused with malt vinegar by the housekeeper Dolly. My mum, and her mother, would have been out earlier, with a bucket and small spade to gather cockles, joining the women from Laugharne and Ferryside who trawled the sands at the extreme point of the estuary called the Ginst, under Sir John's Hill, loading their donkeys with cockles.

Above left to right:
Laugharne Castle;
View across the
Laugharne estuary.

Left: Dylan and
his family on a
Laugharne Ferry.

Next, I wander down the steps, appreciating the dramatic views across the estuary. Mably the dog is close to me, sniffing the rock wall. At the bottom of the steps, I hear a small cry among the bushes, where my mum has hidden her baby brother Colm, terribly jealous of all the attention he is getting. It was a common occurrence for the small baby to go missing, though one day was to prove more memorable for my mum than the others. After placing Colm under a bush, Aeron went off to play with her friends and visited her much-loved Granny Thomas at The Pelican. Together they would draw sheep, using a wavy outline to suggest the woolly

pelt and eat the tops of the numerous rice puddings cooked that day. Hours later, as she returned to the Boathouse, she remembered Colm. Rushing to where she had left him, she found that he was gone! Fortunately, like every other time, he had been quickly found.

I then hear a loud shriek from the outdoor lavatory, pelt down the stairs and get knocked aside by my terrified grandfather rushing into the kitchen, holding up his trousers with one hand, (the other is in a sling) and jumping onto a chair hysterically screaming, "Rats ... Millions of them ... With whiskers ... with a tail a foot long." My mum and grandmother, "the brave

Above: The Boathouse.

ones", would fearlessly chase the (one) rat under the garden shed and I hear my grandmother comment, "You can tell whose daughter you are."

Back in the kitchen, I meet Dolly the housekeeper, or 'the treasure' as the family affectionately knew her. Dolly was in her 20s, with a stock of floral, Vera Lynn dresses. She wore her black hair long and lank over her narrow shoulders; her face was thin and stricken, although according to my mum, after her mother and of course Granny, Dolly was the most beautiful, radiant person she ever knew. I picture her beating clothes to a pulp against a washing board, grumbling that her hands are red raw, complaining she has to do two washdays every week, one here and one at home.

Whilst in the kitchen, I spot Booda, the neighbour and Laugharne's ferryman, drinking a cup of strong tea and eating Welsh cakes, whilst sharing his *Dennis the Menace* comic with Dolly's son, Desmond.

Following a meal of my grandmother's Irish stew for the adults, (which, being a few days old, has changed to a slightly green colour) and egg and chips cooked by Dolly for the children's tea, I see my grandmother preparing Dylan a bath, leaving sweets along the side for him to suck while he sings or speaks in his low mumbled boom bringing the *Under Milk Wood* characters to life. If my mum is quick enough, she catches her father after his bath and I see them comfortably ensconced in a capacious armchair, reading stories and rhymes together. Mum always felt that it was the best time of the week, when her father opened a book with her.

As my grandparents are preparing to go out for the evening, I notice Aeron sneaking out onto the veranda below and she watches the water slowly rising in a moon-shaped pool as it seeps from an opening in the wall, which they call 'the harbour'. Slowly, yet confidently, the sea floods the back garden so the estuary, with tern, gull and heron, and its surrounding countryside, with hawk and sparrow, become their extended garden.

My mother once said about returning to Laugharne, "The funny thing is I find myself going back again and again." We have put this quote on a bench at the Boathouse that overlooks the stunning views of the estuary in memory of Mum. We thought this was appropriate, as not only did my grandfather, grandmother and mother all come back to Laugharne, but now so do the next generations, my son and I keep coming back as well. My son adores climbing the tower in Laugharne Castle and tries to wake the sleeping dragon at the castle entrance or the troll that lives in the secret garden at the back. The fact that it was in the castle grounds that his great-grandfather remembered his childhood and wrote his autobiographical stories in *Portrait of the Artist as A Young Dog*, only adds to the magic of Laugharne, which still continues to ignite the Thomas family's imagination.

Greenwich Village,
Manhattan, New York.

New York Greenwich Village:
Ghostly Echoes on Paper
by Peter Thabit Jones

"I've had **18** STRAIGHT whiskies..."

St. Vincent's Hospital

6th AVENUE

Greenwich Avenue

Patchin Place

8th AVENUE

The Hudson RIVER

White horse TAVERN

E.E.Cummings' apartment

waverly

Bleeker St

christopher st

7th Avenue

West 4th Street

W 4th

W 3rd

Memorial to Dylan Thomas here

Hudson Street

chumley's speak easy

Minetta Tavern

Minetta s

Greenwich st

Bedford Street

Dylan completed Under Milk Wood in New York

church of ST. LUKE in the Fields

Cherry Lane THEATRE

Hotel Chelsea

Hotel EARLE

Washington Square

The Dove

Dylan's first meal in America

Carpo's CAFE

Time passes. Greenwich Village, situated below 14th Street and West of Broadway, has mostly become the neighbourhood of those on the upper middle-class rung of the social ladder.

However, the thoroughly engaging area of New York City, edged by the Hudson River, still pulses with its history of counter-cultures. Beneath the modern commercialisation, it is a place where radical, fresh, vibrant, brave, at times eccentric, movements in literature, art, music, and politics came to life, spreading alternative experiments and visions across America and the rest of the world. One is in a place where the likes of Walt Whitman and Salvador Dalí lived, and where Billie Holiday and Bob Dylan kick-started their careers.

With its green heart of Washington Square Park, it was a retreat for Dylan Thomas, a place where he could relax when not being the self-described "voice on wheels" from New York to California on those tours from 1950 to 1953. He went to 'the Village' for the bars and restaurants, which was a place buzzing with creativity in the 1950s. It was a world away from slowed-down Laugharne, indeed a Britain shadowed by rationing. It was far from a poverty-struck Boathouse, far from his writing shed where he would wait as patient as a heron for the appropriate word.

He went to America as a mature man who had been horrified by the Second World War, the Blitz on London and Swansea. He had worked on propaganda films which expanded his vision, and he was aiming for more clarity in his writing. He arrived in an optimistic and ambitious America, a country that would ascend within several decades to an empirical status, its political and cultural influences impacting on most parts of the globe. The friends he made, who were working in all areas of the arts, were the sons and daughters of this confident nation. They included those living in Greenwich Village, such as sculptor David Slivka and poet E. E. Cummings.

So what was the impact of Greenwich Village, indeed New York with its skyscraper-canyons of carnival-busy days and nights and its rainbow of races, on his actual writing? One must consider three things when it comes to his creative output and America. Firstly, the battle between performer and poet on those demanding tours; secondly, what he did produce and hoped to produce; and, thirdly, what might have been produced had he not died so young.

Caitlin's dislike of his 'escapes' to America to avoid writing is well documented. In a 1952 letter to Madame Caetani, who sponsored the Rome-based magazine *Botteghe Oscure*, he admitted that in America he could only play a poet and not make poetry. He told some correspondents he was unable to get on with writing even when in Laugharne. He did however complete 'Poem on his Birthday' prior to his 1952 trip to America and the publisher New Directions brought out a publication of six new poems, written since 1946, for that tour. In February 1953, he was confessing to being able to just about complete 'Author's Prologue', which prefaced his *Collected Poems*.

So what are his writings connected with Greenwich Village? It is only in his letter writing, to his parents and to Caitlin, that we get a tantalising whiff of what he could have written. His American writings, therefore, are

his 'completion' of *Under Milk Wood*, which he also worked on in Laugharne for its New York premiere, and 'A Visit to America', a brief prose-piece.

Broadcast after his death on BBC radio in March 1954, this is Dylan's only response to America. It is powered by his usual style; a traffic-jam of inventive jokes, an alliterative listing of words, and over-the-top comparisons; in fact his individual and mischievous wonderland of poetic prose.

Under Milk Wood is not only proof that he could focus on a work with a deadline when forced, but also a signpost to one of the creative roads he would have continued along. In March 1953 he was promising John Malcolm Brinnin the complete manuscript of his 'play for voices' on his arrival for his penultimate tour. It was to be performed at the Kaufmann Auditorium in New York. Dylan worked on it in the Hotel Chelsea, at Brinnin's Boston apartment, and in Rollie McKenna's home in Millbrook, New York. He was still making changes on his final tour for his last public performance in October.

What might he have written had he not died? The success of *Under Milk Wood* got him excited about other possibilities. After its first presentation, he told E. F. Bozman of J. M. Dent that he would work on another 'play for voices'. He told Brinnin of his plan to write a "proper-er play". He even talked of a drama

called *Two Streets*. He considered adapting his story 'The Followers' into a radio play.

What if the collaboration with Igor Stravinsky had become a reality? Dylan met Stravinsky and spoke of a work about a world decimated by an atomic bomb and followed by a Garden of Eden-like beginning. Also, his readings had made him realise an audience's initial need for clarity. The groundbreaking recordings with Caedmon Records might have inspired ideas for that medium. Then there are his friendships with some of America's most innovative poets. He suggested to Theodore Roethke in a 1953 letter that they could learn from each other as poets.

It is possible he discussed stretching the rubber band of poetry with Greenwich Village-based Filipino poet, José Garcia Villa, a dear friend who was renowned for his eccentric and excessive use of commas in poems.

Dylan Thomas was the superb master of the Houdini approach to achieving freedom within the strait-jacket of his self-made forms. One wonders where his sound-texturing obsession, his craftsman's need to sing within the chains of his own making, on full display in *Under Milk Wood* and in his final and unfinished poem 'Elegy' would have taken him. What writings would have come from his 'memory bank', widened and deepened by America? Would he have offered the

world poems confronting growing technology and the damage to holy nature? Surely he would have used his skills in pursuing his kind of stage dramas, writing for television and film scripts? I have sometimes wondered if John Lennon and Paul McCartney, fans of Dylan, would have considered him as a scriptwriter for the 1964 Beatles' film *A Hard Day's Night*. Dylan would have been 50 years of age. It was, of course, scripted by Welshman Alun Owen.

Time passes. The name of Dylan Thomas will forever be connected with Greenwich Village. We should cherish the writings we do have because his unique works still have much to offer our ever-changing, complex 'global village'.

Bibliography

Ferris, Paul. 1978. *Dylan Thomas*. Middlesex: Penguin Books Ltd.

Fitzgibbon, Constance. 1966. *Selected Letters of Dylan Thomas*. London: J.M. Dent & Sons Ltd.

Lycett, Andrew. 2004. *Dylan Thomas: A New Life*. London: Phoenix.

Contributors

Phil Carradice is a poet, novelist, historian and broadcaster. He has written over 50 books, including a biography on Dylan Thomas for children. A Fellow of The Welsh Academy, he broadcasts regularly on Radio Wales and BBC Radio 3 and 4.

Hannah Ellis is the granddaughter of Dylan Thomas. A former teacher, she now writes books for children. She was a patron of the Dylan Thomas 100 festival, and is currently the creative consultant for the Dylan Thomas Estate.

Peter Thabit Jones, poet and dramatist, is the author of 13 books, including *Dylan Thomas Walking Tour of Greenwich Village* with Aeronwy Thomas. He was inducted into the Phi Sigma Iota Society at Salem State University, Massachusetts in 2014.

Andrew Lycett has written a number of acclaimed biographies, including one on Dylan Thomas. He is a Fellow of the Royal Society of Literature.

Gillian Clarke has been the National Poet of Wales since 2008 and was awarded the Queen's Gold Medal for Poetry in 2010. Her collection *Ice* was shortlisted for the T. S. Eliot Prize in 2012.

Griff Rhys Jones is a TV actor, writer and producer. He was executive producer of *A Poet in New York* and in 2014 organised the Dylan Thomas in Fitzrovia festival in London.

T. James Jones is a former Archdruid of Wales, a National Eisteddfod crowned and chaired bard and the foremost translator of both Dylan Thomas' poetry and prose into Welsh including *Under Milk Wood (Dan y Wenallt)*.

Robert Minhinnick has twice won the Wales Book of the Year and also the Forward Prize for 'Best Single Poem'. His latest publications include *Island of Lightning* and *Limestone Man*. He is an advisor to the charity Sustainable Wales.

Chris Moss is a travel writer from Lancashire, England. From 2012-2014 he lived in Laugharne and is the author of a book on the cultural history of Patagonia and a guide to the Wales Coast Path.

Berwyn Rowlands is a Welsh internationalist who has many years experience in film and events. In 2006 he established the Iris Prize, the world's largest LGBT short film prize.

Jeff Towns is a rare book-dealer who has specialised in Dylan Thomas materials for over 45 years. He is the former Chair of The Dylan Thomas Society and has written and edited several books about the poet.

Samantha Wynne Rhydderch is a poet. Both her collections from Picador were shortlisted for Wales Book of the Year. In 2014 her pamphlet *Lime & Winter* was published by Rack Press and shortlisted for the Michael Marks Award.

Pascale Petit is a poet. Her poetry collection *Fauverie* was shortlisted for the T. S. Eliot Prize and won the Manchester Poetry Prize. *What the Water Gave Me: Poems after Frida Kahlo* was shortlisted for the T. S. Eliot Prize and Wales Book of the Year.

Peter Stead is a writer and broadcaster who taught History at universities in Wales and America. He is the Founder and President of the International Dylan Thomas Prize.

George Tremlett is a journalist and biographer who runs the Corran Bookshop in Laugharne. He co-wrote *Caitlin: Life with Dylan Thomas* with Caitlin Thomas.

Sarah Edmonds is a Welsh illustrator who creates characters, places and patterns that tell stories. In 2013 she was awarded a summer artist residency with Kultivera in Tranås, Sweden, where her enthusiasm for drawing narrative maps flourished.

Dylan Thomas Timeline

1914

27 October: Dylan Marlais Thomas born at 5 Cwmdonkin Drive, Swansea.

1925

Dylan is a pupil at Swansea Grammar School where his father teaches English.

Dylan's 'Song of a Mischievous Dog' published in the school magazine, which he later edits.

1927

Dylan's poem 'His Requiem' appears in Wales' *Western Mail* newspaper. Over 40 years later it was discovered it had been cribbed from *The Boys Own Paper* of November 1923. It was one of his favourite boyhood reads.

1929

One of Dylan's couplets is quoted in London magazine *Everyman*.

Dylan's essay 'Modern Poetry' is published in the school magazine.

1930

Dylan begins the first of his notebooks containing his poetry.

1931

Dylan leaves school to become a reporter on the South Wales *Daily Post*.

1932

Dylan leaves his job but continues as a freelance journalist.

1933

'And Death Shall Have No Dominion' is published in the *New English Weekly*.

August: Dylan's first visit to London at the age of 19.

1934

Dylan's first visit to Laugharne. Dylan moves to London.

Dylan's first volume of poetry *18 Poems* is published at the age of 20.

1936

Dylan meets Caitlin Macnamara in London.

Dylan's second collection of poems *Twenty-Five Poems* is published.

1937

Dylan makes his first radio broadcast 'Life And The Modern Poet'.

Dylan and Caitlin are married in Penzance, Cornwall.

1938

Dylan begins negotiations for publication of his work in America.

Dylan and Caitlin move to his parents' house in Swansea.

Dylan and Caitlin move to Laugharne.

1939

The couple's first son, Llewelyn, is born.

A collection of poems and prose, *The Map of Love*, is published.

The World I Breathe becomes Thomas' first collection published in America.

1940

Dylan leaves Laugharne to move to London.

Dylan's collection of short stories *Portrait of The Artist as a Young Dog* is published.

Dylan begins writing war propaganda film scripts.

1942

Dylan's poem 'After the Funeral (In Memory of Ann Jones)' is published.

1943

New Poems published.

Dylan's daughter Aeronwy is born in London, named after the Aeron River.

1944

The family moves to Bosham in Sussex.

The family moves to New Quay, Wales.

Dylan records 'Quite Early One Morning' for the BBC Welsh Home Service.

1945

Dylan records 'Memories of Christmas' for the BBC Welsh Service Children's Hour.

1946

Deaths And Entrances which contains 'Fern Hill' is published.

Selected Writings is published in America.

Dylan and family move to Holywell Ford House, Magdalen College in Oxford.

1947

June: Margaret Taylor buys the Manor House in South Leigh, Oxfordshire for the Thomas family.

1948

Dylan stays in Llangain with his father, while Dylan's mother Florence is in hospital.

1949

Dylan and family move to the Boathouse in Laugharne.

Dylan's son Colm is born in Carmarthen Hospital in Wales.

1950

Dylan's first American tour organised by John Malcolm Brinnin.

Twenty Six Poems delivered to the American publisher Dents.

1951

'Do not go gentle into that good night' published in *Botteghe Oscure*.

1952

Second American tour with Caitlin joining him.

Dylan's first recording for Caedmon Records.

'In Country Sleep' is published in America.

Collected Poems 1934-1952 is published.

Dylan's father dies at the age of 76.

1953

April: Dylan's third American tour.

19 October: Leaves for final American tour and delivers *Under Milk Wood* to BBC.

27 October: Dylan's 39th birthday.

Dylan drinks increasingly to cope with stress and worry. He is very ill with bronchial pneumonia. Falls into coma following a doctor's injection.

Caitlin Thomas flies to New York.

November 9: Dylan dies at St Vincent's Hospital, New York aged 39.

Dylan Thomas Bibliography

18 Poems (1934)

Dylan's first collection of poems was published in December 1934, not long after after his 20th birthday.

Twenty-five Poems (1936)

Dylan continued to rework some of his Notebook Poems, written between the ages of 15 and 19, for *Twenty-five Poems*.

The Map of Love (1939)

The Map of Love, a collection of poetry and stories, was published in August 1939, but the book's reception was overshadowed by the build up to war.

The World I Breathe (1939)

This selection of poetry and prose was Dylan's first volume publication in America.

Portrait of the Artist as a Young Dog (1940)

This collection of semi-autobiographical short stories is largely set in Swansea and Carmarthenshire.

New Poems (1943)

Dylan's second volume to be published in America.

Deaths and Entrances (1946)

Deaths and Entrances was instantly popular: a first run of 3,000 was followed by a reprint of a further 3,000 a month later.

Selected Writings (1946)

Another American edition of Dylan's poetry and prose.

In Country Sleep (1952)

This American volume included 'Do not go gentle into that good night'.

Collected Poems 1934 - 1952 (1952)

In his author's note, Dylan wrote: "This book contains most of the poems I have written, and all, up to the present year, that I wish to preserve. Some of them I have revised a little, but if I went on revising everything that I now do not like in this book I should be so busy that I would have no time to try to write new poems."

Collected Poems (1953)

The American edition of Dylan's *Collected Poems*. It was published just before Dylan's third American lecture tour.

The Doctor and the Devils (1953)

This was the first of Dylan's film scripts to be published.

Under Milk Wood (1954)

Dylan's famous 'play for voices' was first read on stage at The Poetry Center in New York on 14 May 1953 and was published after Dylan's death.

Dylan Thomas Bibliography Copyright © 2014 Dylan Thomas Centre, City and County of Swansea www.dylanthomas.com

The National Library of Wales

The National Library of Wales in Aberystwyth holds the largest single collection of Dylan Thomas material in the world. Here, all those interested in his life and work can study the intricate detail of the manuscripts on which he painstakingly composed his poetry. A selection of the drafts, correspondence, doodles and photographs from this vast collection can be viewed on the online Dylan exhibition (dylan.llgc.org.uk), and visitors to the Library can also enjoy the films and voice recordings at the National Screen and Sound Archive.

Useful websites:
www.dylanthomas.com
www.visitwales.com
www.llgc.org.uk

Photography credits

A Dylan Odyssey Calendar 2016

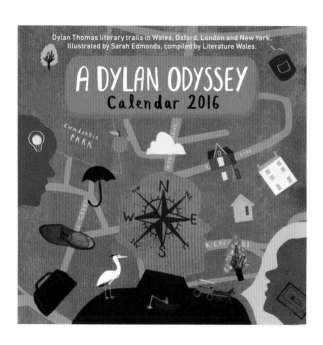

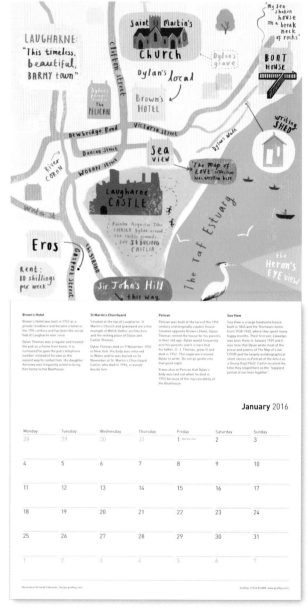

Follow in the footsteps of Dylan Thomas with this calendar featuring 12 literary tour maps and supporting narrative. Enjoy Dylan's favourite locations all year round in this super size engagement calendar. Each month has a different tour with a description of locations associated with Dylan Thomas including: Laugharne, Swansea, Carmarthenshire, New Quay, Gower, Criccieth, Fitzrovia London, Oxford and Greenwich Village New York City.

Title: A Dylan Odyssey Calendar 2016
Item: Wall calendar
ISBN: 9781909823761
Format: size 300 x 300mm
Price: £15.99

Available at bookshops, gifts shops and www.graffeg.com

A Dylan Odyssey Notecard Pack
10 Cards and Envelopes

Ten illustrated notecards in a gift pack, with literary tour maps. Send a message with one of Dylan's favourite locations.

Each card has a different tour with a description of locations associated with Dylan Thomas including: Laugharne, Swansea, Carmarthenshire, New Quay, Gower, Criceith, Fitzrovia London, Oxford and Greenwich Village New York City.

Title: A Dylan Odyssey Notecard Pack
Item: 10 Notecards and envelopes
ISBN: 9781909823891
Format: size 160 x 160mm
Price: £12.99

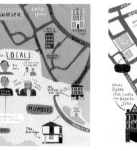

153

Dylan Thomas Notecards

A unique series of notecards with some of Dylan's most memorable lines from his poetry, short stories and letters. The pack of notecards has 10 different quotations, with room inside for a message. Suitable for any occasion. Gift pack contains 10 individual cards and envelopes.

Title: Dylan Thomas Notecard Pack
Item: 10 Notecards and envelopes
ISBN: 9781909823587
Format: cards size 160 x 120mm
Price: £7.99

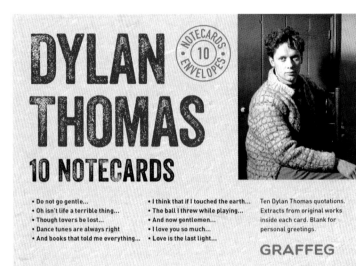

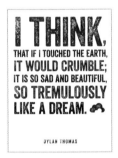

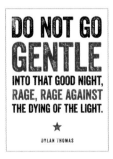

Available at bookshops, gifts shops and www.graffeg.com

Poster Poem collection revival

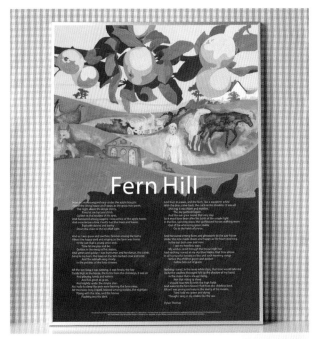

Cofio **Waldo Williams £12.99**
ISBN 9781909823679

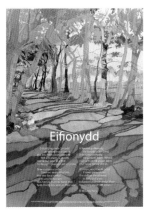

Eifionydd **R. Williams Parry**
£12.99 ISBN 9781909823839

Fern Hill **Dylan Thomas £12.99**
ISBN 9781909823624

Return to Cardiff **Dannie Abse**
£12.99 ISBN 9781909823648

'Fern Hill' by Dylan Thomas is one of a series of 6 Poster Poems illustrated by Sue Shields, first published by the Welsh Arts Council in the 70's. Graffeg is republishing this popular collection of poster poems, also as notecard gift packs and small gift books. Posters are a standard frame size 700 x 500mm and gift packed in labelled tubes.

Title: Fern Hill Poster Poem
Item: Poster Poem
ISBN: 9781909823624
Format: size 700 x 500mm
Price: £12.99

Title: Fern Hill Poem Book
Item: Poem Book
ISBN: 9781909823846
Format: hardback 24 pages
size 150 x 150mm
Price: £4.99

Hon **T.H. Parry Williams £12.99**
ISBN 9781909823655

Maggie fach **Idris Davies £12.99**
ISBN 9781909823815

Literary Tours in Wales

"...a truly spectacular day that
will live long in my memory..."

Photo ©Hannah Lawson

**Why not go on a literary
adventure of your own?**
Literature Wales runs one-off
literary tours every summer.

Visit **www.literaturewales.org**
for more information or contact
post@literaturewales.org
029 2047 2266 / @LitWales

Llenyddiaeth
Cymru
Literature
Wales

Tour Notes

Tour Notes

Tour Notes

Acknowledgements

Graffeg would like to thank all the contributors who wrote essays for this book: Hannah Ellis, Phil Carradice, Gillian Clarke, Berwyn Rowlands, Jeff Towns, T. James Jones, Pascale Petit, Griff Rhys Jones, Peter Stead, George Tremlett, Samantha Wynne-Rhydderch, Robert Minhinnick, Andrew Lycett, Chris Moss and Peter Thabit Jones. Graffeg would also like to thank the staff at Literature Wales for their inspiration behind the project, for compiling the content, and for their ongoing support, diligence and enthusiasm.

The editor and publisher are also grateful to Jeff Towns for his major contribution in researching photographs and illustrations and for granting permission to reproduce these. We are also grateful to estate holders and publishers for permissions to include selected articles, prose and writings, photographs, illustrations and printed ephemera; we thank them for their cooperation in the preparation of this book. We would also like to thank illustrator Sarah Edmonds for her amazing maps for each chapter and her special titles lettering.

Every effort has been made to trace copyright holders and to obtain their permission for the use of copyright material. The publisher apologizes for any errors or omissions and would be grateful for notification of any corrections that should be incorporated in future reprints or editions of this book.

Lastly the publishers would like to thank the Welsh Government, Arts Council of Wales and the Welsh Books Council for their advice, encouragement and financial support.